Cántaro
Institute

INAUGURAL ADDRESS (1926)

The Significance of the Law-Idea for the Science and Philosophy of Law

Collected Works
Series B, Volume 13

Author: **Herman Dooyeweerd** Series Editor: **Danie F. M. Strauss**

INAUGURAL ADDRESS (1926)

The Significance of the Law-Idea for the Science and Philosophy of Law

Collected Works
Series B, Volume 13

Author: **Herman Dooyeweerd**   Series Editor: **Danie F. M. Strauss**

cantaroinstitute.org

Inaugural Address (1926): The Significance of the Law-Idea for the Science and Philosophy of Law

Collected Works of Herman Dooyeweerd
Series Editor: Danie F. M. Strauss
Volume Editor: Harry Van Dyke, Alan Cameron

Book Design: Steven R. Martins

ISBN 978-1-998711-36-9

Printed in the United States of America

INAUGURAL ADDRESS
(1926)

*The Significance of the Law-Idea for the Science
and Philosophy of Law*

CONTENTS

Foreword

This study functioned as Dooyeweerd's inaugural oration upon assuming the office of Professor of Law in the Free University of Amsterdam on October 15, 1926. It is not known how much of it he actually read on that occasion, but he published it that same year as an integral text in a separate booklet of 112 pages.

In view of its length and its four chief subdivisions, it seemed more reader-friendly to publish a translation of this rich text in book form, in which the author's subheadings are converted into chapter headings. Sections in the text introduced by the word **Remark** contain significant passages that were originally tucked away in lengthy endnotes but have here been retrieved and placed in the main text, where they shed further light on the discussion at that point.

A draft translation of this work was first prepared by the late Dr. Phil Brouwer and reviewed and edited by Harry Van Dyke. Any editorial annotation appears in brackets.

A note about terminology: the term *wetsidee* used in this text of 1926 is translated as "law-idea," even though thirty years later Dooyeweerd chose to have it rendered as "cosmonomic idea," given the intended scope of the term. To distinguish *wetsidee* from *rechtsidee* (which too can be translated as law-idea), the latter will be translated as "idea of law." Finally, the term *juridisch* used in this early text has been rendered as "jural," even though in later publications it would in most contexts be replaced by "juridical."

Summer 2025
D. F. M. Strauss

INTRODUCTION

During the 17th century a perceptive thinker wondered: Why is it that logical thought has achieved such incontrovertible and universally accepted results in the realm of mathematical science, whereas in the areas of religion, politics, ethics, and legal theory a battleground remains for the most contradictory views and conceptions, all seeking recognition as absolute truth?

His answer? That's because truth and human interests do not clash in the field of mathematics, but the moment reason claims sovereign validity in religion, morality and law it evokes instinctive resistance and adamant contradiction. "For as oft as reason is against a man, so oft will a man be against reason."[1]

It's a curious conclusion indeed, one that opens much more profound perspectives than our author himself would have suspected from the vantage point of his humanistic rationalism. For here one encounters, no doubt against the intention of the writer [Thomas Hobbes], the stark internal contradiction, the inner antinomy which like a spiritual disease permeates an entire genre of world and life views, regardless of their multicolored variety.

Indeed, mankind did have an overriding and all-encompassing interest in halting the triumphal march of mathematical thought which humanism had enthroned. It needed to be stopped before it would also conquer the domain of man's loftiest, most sacred, and most personal affairs. What is more, humanism itself—and that is the crux of the antinomy I wish to point out—was necessarily divided against itself and torn apart by the battle-cry of the sovereignty of reason.

The aggressive slogan of the sovereignty of reason, the maxim of the irresistible force of methodical thought, received its most forceful stimulus from a motive quite irrational: namely, the humanistic ideal of personality. This ideal, starting with the Renaissance and its initial attack on the Scholastic order of life, had already been proclaimed the harbinger of a new future.

What we have here is an irreconcilable dualism: *the ideal of personality*—of the *uomo universale*, the free, regal human person who was to take charge of the world and who, in his own sovereign creative urge, would determine his own attitude toward life—this ideal impelled reason to break down the entire natural worldview and then reconstruct it, out of nothing as it were, into a logical structure of its own making.

All of nature, from the mechanical motion of so-called inanimate matter to mysterious organic life, fell prey to the analyzing, mathematical mode of thought. The fundamental idea of the humanistic *ideal of science* demanded continuity of thought and insisted that all newly acquired knowledge be founded in its logical origin, requiring the creation of a continuous coherence of the elements of knowledge, unfettered by any irrational limits.[2] But as soon as the problem of the soul, the bearer of the new ideal of life, cropped up, the inner antinomy of the humanistic world and life view, namely the irresolvable conflict between the ideal of science and the ideal of personality, was inevitably exposed for all to see.

The ideal of science, if unchecked in its relentless drive for continuity, was bound to subdue the new sovereign, the human personality. It was bound to destroy man's moral freedom and his illusion of grandeur, and to lay bare the laws according to which personality develops slavishly, like a mechanism.

Indeed, man himself had an eminent interest in limiting the sovereignty of mathematical thought. But where to find these limits, and how to delimit the competencies, respectively, of science and personality? The evil spirit of sovereign thought, the logical postulate of continuity, had itself been conjured up by the humanistic ideal of personality, and so humanism had every reason to exclaim, with Faust: "*Die ich rief, die Geister, werde ich jetzt nicht los*": The spirits I have summoned I can no longer escape.[2a]

The bitter debates between Thomas Hobbes (1588–1679) and René Descartes (1596–1650) embodied the antinomy, the dualism, of the humanistic world and life view. Two great thinkers, sharing an enthusiastic faith in the new ideal of science and suffused with the spirit of the humanistic ideal of personality, carried on a fierce battle about the limits of the new method of science.

Descartes capitulated before the irrational requirements of the ideal of personality. Like Hobbes, he energetically applied the mathematical-mechanistic method to the entire field of inorganic and organic nature, demolished the Aristotelian-Thomistic conception of substantial forms, but called a halt before the soul, the bearer of personality. He juxtaposed soul and body as two independent "substances" that are not related to each other in any way.

Hobbes, by contrast, infatuated with the ideal of continuity in the form of Galileo's mathematical concept of science, would admit no limits that could restrict the mathematical method. What judge could decide on the *actio finium regundorum*—on how to define the boundaries? Once the sovereignty of reason is accepted, its claim to superiority must be taken seriously. In Hobbes, body and motion are the basic denominators to which all phenomena of both nature and spirit must be reduced if they are to be amenable to the computations of mathematical logic. In the concept of *conatus* (impulse) the continuity was safeguarded in motion itself.

If law and state are indeed to be founded, mathematically, on eternal, immutable principles of reason, as the natural-law theory of humanism had claimed since Grotius (1583–1645), then, in line with Plato's requirement, the hypothesis that is to serve as the starting point in the chain of natural-law deductions must first be logically accounted for, and the first thing to be established is the logical coherence between the mechanical-mathematical laws of motion and the laws governing law and state. There you have the program of continuity, whose execution requires that the areas of "being" and "ought" be brought into a unitary logical coherence by the mathematical creative method. In Spinoza's monism, law and power became identical; in a materialist fashion it drew the ultimate inference from the ideal of science.

That is how the inner antinomy in the foundations of the humanistic world and life view gained its first, somewhat crude, shape in the struggle between Descartes' "idealism" and Hobbes' "materialism."

No deeper fundamental division separated these humanists. Idealism and materialism are but polar tensions within the same vision of life and the world—tensions between a personality ideal and a science ideal. Almost imperceptibly, idealism and materialism could pass the one into the other.

This inner tension underwent a major refinement in the philosophy of Leibniz, which sought to reconcile the two ideals by conceiving a compromise between the mathematical-mechanistic view of the world and the teleological-organic conception of life. In the concept of "function" Leibniz's differential and integral calculus provided an extremely fruitful and well-honed instrument by which, in the course of numerous imperceptible transitions, the universe could be recreated to constitute a continuous logical unity. This gave the *law of continuity*, the fundamental law of humanistic rationalism, its classic formulation. It dissolved the universe into an infinite number of monads (non-spatial, animated points of force which, without materially affecting each other, each on its own, reflect the entire universe by the representation in the fundamental law of continuity), while still retaining the universe as a continuous coherence by *harmonia praestabilita*, the principle of predetermined harmony.

The concept of function, which caused discrete number and continuous space to flow (logically, not materially) into each other by way of creative motion in an infinite series of transitions, was able to rescue continuity without denying the unbridgeable qualitative difference between soul and body, the realm of natural reality and that of the dignity of personality. Leibniz's theory of unconscious representation was based on the idea of continuity. In its deeper metaphysical sense, as a principle of general order (*principium quoddam generale*) originating in infinity, the law of continuity could only be based directly on the *harmonia praestabilita*, the eternal order of the cosmos. Leibniz himself saw the eternal *harmonia praestabilita* as the origin of the law of continuity.

Remark: See Leibniz's *Gesammelte Werke* (1843–47), IV, 129, 199. In contradistinction to the entelechy view of continuity found in Scholasticism, a classic formulation of the law of continuity is found in a Postscript intended for De Volder in a letter of Leibniz to Bernoulli, dated 30 Sept. 1698; in *Gesammelte Werke*, III, 544:

For otherwise that great and it seems to me inviolable axiom that governs nature, which I was perhaps the first to notice, would not be observed. I recently made an original use of it in the *Nouvelles de la République des Lettres*, and I call it the law of continuity. When I objected to Huygens' support for axioms, a year or so before his death, he admitted that the law of continuity was worth considering. It states that in changes there are no leaps, and consequently, that there is no assignable change in an instant, and likewise that it is impossible to pass from motion to rest, or to motion in the opposite direction, or vice versa, except through intermediate places. Hence, those who maintain (as indeed everyone commonly does) that motion never happens through leaps or that a body cannot pass from one place to another, have seen the truth, but not the whole truth. For the same thing is observed no less in changes of degree than in changes of place.

The deeper coherence between Leibniz's rationalistic view of the law of continuity and his metaphysical law-idea of *pre-established harmony* (*harmonia praestabilita*) is ably explained by Herman Schmalenbach in his work *Leibniz* (1921), pp. 452ff.:

> The continuity principle is, precisely in that further sense, a "principle of general order." It derives from "the law of order," in which we of course recognize the "harmony." Fact is, the pre-established harmony is the general foundation, indeed the necessary condition, both for space as mere positional space (i.e., for space as the totality of positional relations) and for the continuity of space. Even if the actual emergence of the continuum should come about from motion, the latter still does not provide the foundation of the existent continuum except on condition that not only the motion of the monads that underlie existence is continuous, but, in addition, that these monads, being internally set in motion, are exactly correlated with each other in a pre-established harmony. The unceasing pre-established harmonious motion of the qualitative positional relations and their abstractly quantitative expression, and then also the abstract totality of these positional relations, abstracted from supposedly frozen motion, can

be regarded as continuous, despite the discontinuity of the positional elements. This obtains when on the one hand the basis of change within each monad is continuous (or in any case must be assumed to be continuous), and on the other hand when the relation of the positional elements before all else continues to conform to compossibility—a compossibility which, like functionalism, is an abstract expression (one that is cognate, indeed identical, with the latter) of the "general order," i.e. of the harmony. (p. 453)

See also Leibniz, *Monadologie*, 47: "God alone is the primitive unity, or the simple original substance, which produces all the created or derivative monads, which are born, so to speak, by *continual fulgurations* of the divinity from moment to moment, limited by the receptivity of the creature, the essence of which to be limited" (ital. added).

On this very point, however, Schmalenbach's exposition of Leibniz's metaphysics, in which he claims to discover the deepest religious root of Calvinist "quantitative individualism" (!), is spoiled and marred by an almost bizarre desire to construe meaning. How can one possibly regard the world and life view of Calvinism as a mathematical, quantitative individualism, considering that its entire structure is characterized by a strong view of the sovereign will of God, a limiting idea of the law, a rejection of every theodicy, and an organic view of life as a whole? And how can one reach such a conclusion on the basis of a superficial historical argument, brushing aside the *antithetic* position of Leibniz's law-idea vis-à-vis that of Calvinism, an antithesis which does not merely touch upon the periphery but penetrates to the very heart, to the vital center, of both systems, signifying a "to be or not to be" for both of them? These misunderstandings can be understood only in terms of a peculiar trait of many humanistic approaches to history: in this domain, too, they follow the continuity bias, resulting in re-interpreting the differences in principle between life-and-world views as merely relative.

This bias of humanism is best portrayed by the words of Dilthey: "Not the relativity of every worldview is the last word of the Spirit that has traversed them all, *but the sovereignty of the Spirit toward each and every one of them*, and at the same time the positive awareness how in the Spirit's diverse manifestations the one world presents itself to us, and that the enduring types of worldview are the expression of the many-sidedness of the world." [3]

To illustrate Schmalenbach's way of writing history, it may suffice to mention that according to him the absolutistic "bureaucratic state" is a product of the Calvinist ethos (*sic*). He substantiates this claim with a misplaced reference to Max Weber in terms of which he views the capitalistic production system as a product of, of all things, the Calvinist ethics (op. cit., p. 232).

Leibniz's system displays the basic antinomy of every humanistic world and life view between the science-ideal and the personality ideal in an extremely delicate complexity. The personality ideal already exhibits the rudimentary trait of the *Aufklärung* (*Enlightenment*) and in this sense is indeed quantitative individualistic. In a most complex intertwinement the arithmetical element, the discreteness of the universe, is metaphysically linked with this personalistic individualism, such that one indeed acquires a view on the antinomy of continuity and discreteness, on the antinomy of the transfinite, and thus may appreciate the peculiar symbolic form in which the basic antinomy between science-ideal (continuity ideal) and personality ideal (here still antithetically the individuality ideal) appears in the thought of Leibniz.

It would be extremely important to look at Leibniz's view of state and law by tracing the inner tension between personal freedom and the idea of the police state. Such an investigation would have to commence with Leibniz's view of the *Civitas Dei*, the city of God. On this point, the study of Erwin Ruck, *Die Leibniz'sche Staatsidee* (1909), would have to be revised and amended in a significant way.

[End of the Remark]

In Leibniz, the Spinoza-like formula, *"deus sive natura"* (God or Nature) becomes: *"Harmonia universalis id est Deus"* (Universal harmony, that is God).[4] Despite his central position as all-encompassing monad, God is subject to the law.

The crowning glory of humanistic metaphysics, then, is a rationalistic theodicy, a justification of world history, a reconciliation of evil reality and the ethical ideal. The logos created by sovereign reason, which seemed to resolve all antinomy according to the law of continuity, coincides with the fundamental law of the divine cosmic plan.

Humanistic reason, however, overreached itself. Its focus remained glued to mathematical thought, and the humanistic ideal of science continued to be accorded primacy, as opposed to the humanistic ideal of personality.

The father of critical philosophy, Immanuel Kant (1724–1804) was merciless in laying bare the antinomies in Leibniz's rationalism. Pure ideas, regulative principles of reason quite removed from possible experience, had been hypostatized to constitute a metaphysical reality. Reason, for example, had constructed proofs of the discreteness and infinity of the cosmos as well as of moral freedom and the existence of God. But with the same degree of assumed apodictical certainty, that same reason could be turned around to "prove" the opposite. No arbiter could, purely intellectually, decide between the claims of rationalistic idealism and the claims of materialism, since both systems had misused reason as an intellectual function by overstepping its limits and constructing proofs in thin air.[5]

Nature is constructed as a law-conforming coherence by means of man-made categories of the understanding and forms of apprehension. These categories of the understanding, however, always depend on apprehension, on sensory experience. If the understanding applies its powers to the hidden meaning of the creation apart from all experience it can only build airy castles and is bound to ensnare itself in antinomies from which there is no escape.

Meanwhile, what the understanding alone is not able to achieve (namely, to discover absolute truths apart from experience) is precisely what the higher function of the consciousness of reason is irresistibly driven to do. The understanding can only order the presentations, pre-formed by the forms of apprehension of space and time in a chain of cause and effect. And so it finds itself on a never-ending road of determination and closer determination. The natural chain of causality never ends; the understanding never grasps the universe as a well-rounded whole; it is never in a position to call a halt to the infinite series of causes and effects in order to ascend to a final cause, a higher purpose, to God the Creator.

In its ideas, however, reason—still according to Kant—has at its command a means for rising above the infinite relativity of natural reality to the absolute realm of moral values. While the understanding stays with the endless chain of causality, reason, with its ideas, acts as though that chain were completed; it operates with the ideas of first cause, moral freedom, the godhead, and the immortality of the soul. Accordingly, reason automatically ascends beyond the realm of natural reality toward the realm of moral and religious norms. The moral will itself becomes freedom, first cause, autonomous lawgiver, the categorical imperative.

Sein and *Sollen*, the "is" and the "ought," the realm of reality and the realm of personal freedom, the realm of natural laws and moral norms—in other words, the ideal of science and the ideal of personality—are separated by an absolute boundary and lie in totally different dimensions. The understanding is lawgiver in the realm of nature, while reason is the lawgiver in the realm of freedom.

Henceforth, science was to carry through its continuity principle in a strictly positivistic manner in the entire domain that is accessible to sensory experience. The whole world of science and academic scholarship thus came to be identified with mathematical natural science. Meanwhile, alongside this continuity principle—or rather, above and beyond it—moral philosophy, legal philosophy, and religion would be able to maintain the absoluteness of moral and legal values. In Kant, there is no real bridge connecting the realm of nature to the realm of moral values. See the characteristic place in the *Kritik der praktischen Vernunft*:

> The determination of the causality of beings in the world of the senses, as such, can never be unconditioned; and yet for every series of conditions there must be something unconditioned, and therefore there must be a causality which is determined wholly by itself. Accordingly, the idea of freedom as a faculty of absolute spontaneity was not found to be a want, but *as far as its possibility is concerned,* an analytic principle of pure speculative reason. But as it is absolutely impossible to find in experience any example in accordance with this idea, because amongst the causes of things as phenomena, it would be impossible to meet with any absolutely unconditioned determination of causality, we were able to *defend our assumption* that a freely acting cause might be a being in the world of sense, insofar as it is considered from the other point of view as a *noumenon,* only by showing that there is no contradiction in regarding all its actions as subject to physical conditions insofar as they are

phenomena, and yet regarding its causality as physical-
ly unconditioned insofar as the acting being is a being
endowed with understanding and thus making the concept of freedom the regulative principle of reason. By
this principle I do not indeed recognize what the object
is to which that sort of causality is attributed; but I do
remove the difficulty; for, on the one hand, in the explanation of events in the world, and consequently also of
the actions of rational beings, I do justice to the mechanism of physical necessity to go back from conditioned
to conditionality *ad infinitum,* while on the other hand I
keep open for speculative reason the place that is vacant
for it, namely, the intelligible, in order to transfer the
unconditioned thither.

To be sure, in his *Kritik der Urteilskraft* Kant did try to
bring about a synthesis between "*Sein*" and "*Sollen*," between
nature and freedom,[6] just as he sought to order the realm of
culture from the viewpoint of moral ends when developing
his views about the task of philosophy of history. Yet a sober
analysis of the two parts of the Kantian system bears out that
there can be no question here of a genuine reconciliation or
a real synthesis of the two worlds. For Kant, history as an
object of science remains a process which, in its step-by-step
unfolding, is entirely subject to the laws of natural necessity,
of causality. Only a philosophy of history which considers
the human being in historical development as *homo noumenon* can effectively view him as a member of the supra-senso-
ry realm of freedom. But then the history of culture becomes
nothing but the history of the antagonism between nature

and freedom. In this way the independence, the sovereignty, of the historical realm is denied rather than established. It is an unfounded interim sphere between causal nature and the idea of freedom, between the empirical and the noumenal world.

In his *Kritik der teleologischen Urteilskraft*, on the other hand, Kant did attempt to indicate the teleological principle as a subjective mode for the consideration of nature, and he tried to argue that reason is *a priori* compelled and justified in that. Most emphatically, however, he himself claims that this is but a heuristic, regulative principle, which, in approaching the limiting concept of organic life, must guide the causal, mechanistic explanation of nature in discovering the causal coherence which gives rise to the organism.[7] Such a subjective principle, after all, can hardly serve as an encompassing synthetic principle. Nor could the *Kritik der aesthetische Urteilskraft*, which, in terms of Kant's faculty psychology, lays bare the *a priori* forms of feeling as the synthesis of the faculty of representation and the faculty of desire, succeed in providing such a synthetical principle. Schiller and Humboldt's neo-humanism was to elaborate on this "Kritik" later.

Undoubtedly primacy was accorded to practical reason, to the idea of freedom. The postulate requiring that the realm of nature be ordered under the realm of freedom was put forward, but, since the two worlds were not organically reconciled, Kant's world and life view remained dualistically broken despite his *Kritik der Urteilskraft*.

Did this critical dualism, this simply unreconciled conception of two worlds, resolve the inner basic antinomy of the humanistic world and life view? Not at all! One can artfully isolate the worlds of the "is" and the "ought" from each other—one may, next to, or (axiologically) above, nature's law of causality, posit a legal and a moral idea unrelated to that of causality—nevertheless, life, the great cosmic unity by which the human being is bodily and spiritually enveloped, requires a deeper, a real, a cosmic unity. Otherwise the idea of morality with its absolute norms will fade into a *fata morgana*, an idle illusion lacking any possibility of application to reality.

Still worse, the antinomies were not removed, no matter how much Kant had tried to undo them by his critical method. They remained attached to humanism no matter in which direction it sought to rid itself of them. Students of the science of law were to discover this when they attempted to apply Kant's critical method to their field of scholarship. Science, according to Kant, was only possible as empirical natural science. There lies the rub for the science of law which could not, after all, relinquish its claim to scientific status or deny its empirical character if it were not, with Kant and pre-Kantian rationalism, to wind up with mere natural law alone.

A critical position on the pattern of Kant, if it were to apply the critical method fully, would only be able to maintain the science of law as a sociology that seeks to anchor legal phenomena like a causal chain in the continuous structure of the law-conformity of nature according to the method of natural science. So doing it would obviously run into an untenable antinomy with the inescapably normed character of positive law.

The inner dialectics of the humanistic world and life view could not find rest in this phase either.

The primacy of the ideal of personality, which had reached an impasse in Kant's critical dualism, ultimately demanded the removal of this dualism, an identity philosophy of freedom.

Fichte's idealism of freedom represented the first lap on this route. It was in the "*Vernunft*" itself, in reason, that the principle unifying nature and freedom would have to be discovered. This absolute principle is the absolute idea of purpose which Kant had discovered in the realm of freedom. If the various functions of reason are to be deduced, then they will have to be understood as the necessary means in the service of the ultimate goal of reason's activity. All pure forms of reason, deduced separately by Kant, together constitute a teleological system determined by a final goal, a supreme end. Such a system is only possible when the total being, or reason, is sought in an activity that is at work for the sake of a purpose found within itself. But then, as could be expected, the fundamental antinomy of the humanistic world and life view would now be situated in the activity of reason itself.

By its postulate of identity Fichte's theory had been forced to accept an original antagonism in its concept of reason, an antagonism between the ethical goal which reason had set for itself and the activity which seeks to achieve that goal. The basis of all reality had been placed in the ideal of personality and that represents the insoluble antinomy of

Fichte's philosophy of identity.

The concept of *Sollen*, the central concept of Fichte's philosophy, could only take this central place by absorbing the antinomy between nature and freedom, the ideal of science and the ideal of personality, while the theory of science on which Fichte wished to base the identity of science ideal and personality ideal could take no other form than that of antinomic dialectics. Consequently, reason could no longer, as in Kant, be a static given, since it had to create itself in a dialectical manner. All thinking is determined by the principle of pure consciousness: the absolute I creates itself. To create itself it must first distinguish itself from all else and present that to itself as Non-I. "*Das Ich setzt das Nicht-ich im Ich.*" "The I puts the non-I into the I." [8] Here, in theoretical philosophy, we have nature as the product of freedom, as a product of reason's activity, but it is the product of antinomy, of contradiction.

And to save absoluteness, the freedom of the first act of creation not determined by laws, the creation of the "non-I in the I," had to be qualified as an unconscious representation.

Fichte's freedom idealism, which needed dialectics, the method of antinomy, as sovereign method by which to push the old logistic ideal of science back in favor of moral freedom, deeply affected Romanticism. Friedrich Schlegel and Novalis stated openly that the *principium contradictionis* was a thing of the past, that all of life was based on antinomies so as not to be understandable by the principle of formal logic. Personality itself, the idea of moral freedom, must be imported into nature.[9]

History, the mysterious organic operation of moral values in reality, began to charm and fascinate romanticism after the disillusionment of the French Revolution in which the rationalizing, mechanistic theory of natural law proved a complete failure.

There was a longing to reach out beyond Kant's bourgeois ethics of law, his sober concept of duty, towards a loftier, wider, and more liberal view of personality.[10]

The historical school of jurisprudence, brilliantly led by Friedrich Karl von Savigny (1779–1861), formulated its program against the rationalistic hybris of the school of natural law. In the meantime, the inner dialectic of the humanistic world and life view continued on its fatal course.[11]

It led from Kant's dualistic critique to Fichte's freedom idealism, through Schelling to Hegel's philosophy of absolute identity, from subjective to objective idealism. Beyond Fichte's absolute I, the subjective *Vernunft* (reason) required the termination of the humanistic ideal of personality in the *Weltvernunft* (universal reason), the reason of the community. In the unity of absolute substantial thought, in the unity of universal reason, all antinomies, according to Hegel, would be overcome by way of antinomy itself. In eternal logical-metaphysical movement, the uninterrupted dialectical unfolding from thesis to antithesis and synthesis, the humanistic ideal of personality would be elevated to supra-personal substantial thought, to the identity of thought and being in the absolute *Vernunft*. In Hegel, the categories are no longer the pure forms of the understanding, as in Kant, but, rather, the objective configurations of the life of the world itself, in which the Idea discloses itself through its self-unfolding. The ideas have become immanent to the world.

The Idea, as totality of the categories of thought, the realm of the highest moral freedom, posits its own antithesis, the Idea in its otherness, nature. From external nature pure thought (the Idea) returns to itself as *Geist*, as spirit, as personality, synthesis, the unity of the idea and nature. But the spirit, personality itself, immediately re-enters the dialectical self-movement of reason. Initially it is the spirit of the individual, the human being as such, subjective spirit. This is the phase in which personality, the I, stands over against the world and other personalities. Anti-thetically the personality becomes objective spirit, the spirit as it discloses itself in social institutions and world history.

From there the dialectical movement of thought leads to synthesis, the absolute Spirit, in which the objective spirit has been absorbed and elevated into the subjective human spirit.[12]

The state in its historical course of development is the highest realization of absolute Spirit, the mortal God, the realm of the highest moral freedom, while in philosophy the Spirit becomes conscious of itself and learns to know the fundamental dialectical law according to which it realizes itself in nature, law, and the state. In this identity philosophy then, all that is real becomes rational to the extent that it is taken up in the dialectical, circular movement from and to absolute Reason. Value and reality, norms and facts: along the road of antinomy they are brought to a higher synthesis.

There is no longer any conflict, therefore, between the Machiavellian principle of *raison d'état* and abstract natural law; the two have been brought to a synthesis in the dialectical development of world history.[13] By its dialectical principle, identity philosophy relativizes the basic laws of logic itself! It is the antinomy infinitely multiplied in dialectical development!

That, my readers, in broad outline, sketches the basic antinomy of the humanistic world and life view in its historical development, up to and including Hegel. Now I should like to pause and briefly consider the deepest cause of this antinomy. Once we grasp it, we shall begin to see why an endless series of new antinomies had to ensue from this murky source, causing the science of law and legal philosophy to become the battleground of the most contradictory schools of thought. Knowledge of the cause will familiarize us with an idea of immense value, the *law-idea*. Regardless of the many variations in the conceptual elaboration of humanism's law-idea, reflecting on its basic antinomy will prompt us to consider its antithesis with the law-idea proper to the Christian world and life view. Our worldview is in need of closer definition, for the Christian law-idea is decisive for your and my outlook on life, the pulse-beat of our daily activity, and the powerful engine of our academic work at this university.

CHAPTER 1

THE NATURE OF ANTINOMIES

A N ANTINOMY or inner contradiction is not just a contrast, but essentially it is a clash of laws. Justice and injustice, truth and falsehood, virtue and vice are contraries, not antinomies or clashes of laws.[1]

An antinomy arises only when two spheres of law clash with each other: when, for example, the natural law of the necessary relation between cause and effect attacks the validity of ethical norms, or when psychological law-conformity is transformed into a mechanistic one, or when the laws of the jural sphere are reinterpreted as the laws of morality, of the psychical life, of mathematical logic, of pure sociology, or of biology.

Antinomies therefore presuppose a multiplicity of distinct law-spheres. The world and life view, if it is not to entangle itself in numerous antinomies and thereby become useless both for determining one's outlook on life and one's scholarly [scientific] attitude, must seek a competent judge who will indicate, at least in principle, the boundaries between the spheres of validity of the various laws and still integrate the various spheres of law into an organically coherent higher unity.[2]

The basic problem of every world and life view is to account for the origin and mutual coherence of the various law-spheres. This most fundamental problem takes the form of an ineradicable quest for the law-idea which points beyond the confusing multiplicity of law-spheres, beyond the colorful plurality of spheres of life and aspects of the world, to the higher Judge who created the cosmos out of chaos and light out of darkness.

Thus, it is our desire—or rather, in the interest of the purity of our Calvinist world and life view and in the interest of the purity and independence of our Calvinist scholarship, it is our duty—to penetrate to the law-idea in which the deepest tendencies, the innermost promptings of the humanistic world and life view, despite all the seemingly unbridgeable differences in its further elaboration, converge, as it were, in a single focal point.

We then find that the deepest root of the humanistic law-idea is a faith in the sovereignty of personality. This ideal of personality, this irrational foundation, conceived of naturalistically and individualistically during the Italian Renaissance, became in the neo-humanism of Herder, Lessing, Humboldt and Schiller the normative idea of Humanity writ large, the idea of the community of mankind, the utter limit to which the ideal of humanity can elevate itself.[3] As we saw above, this personality ideal also stimulated the humanistic science ideal as the ideal of controlling the world by human thought. All the same, neither the personality ideal nor the science ideal can serve as impartial judge in determining the limits of competence between the law-spheres. Thought and personality are both subordinate to their laws.

If reason is declared sovereign, then, irrevocably, the basic tendency of continuity begins to operate in the field of science and academic scholarship, with the aim to obfuscate whatever limits might obtain for scientific conceptualization. For where *that which is given* is accepted, there the sovereignty of thought is broken. One of the leaders of the Marburg School of neo-Kantians, Paul Natorp, gave classic expression to this basic law of continuity when he said that "from now on there are no longer any conceptual barriers that may not be crossed. Only the procedure itself of this justified border crossing can be called absolute" [4] This basic law may appear in the primitive materialistic shape found in Hobbes, where everything is reduced to motion and matter, while the mechanical laws become the absolutistic monarchs in all areas of law. Or the idea of continuity may appear in idealistic form. Then the concept of function will serve to create a logical continuity for all the categories of the various sciences, while once again the law of one specific sphere becomes the sole mistress of all science.

This introduces a well-nigh endless series of antinomies, some of which we wish to examine in the context of the science of law and legal philosophy.

These antinomies crop up, not just when we approach the limits of personality, but at the very start, in mathematics and logic.[5] Whenever law-limits are ignored for the sake of continuity, thinking will show inherent conflicts between the laws of different spheres thus violated.

The sovereignty of thought, therefore, with its fundamental continuity drive, is a foundation of the humanistic law-idea, but its composition is volcanic and tends to upset the very law-idea itself.

The ideal of personality, however, is no more competent to serve as supreme judge for determining the limits of law. In the so-called humanities it can only cause confusion by relativizing all values that do not as such accord with the idea of sovereign personality, thus destroying them as absolute values. *A certain tendency toward continuity is inherent also in the personality ideal.*

Absolute domination by the ideal of personality causes the ordinances of law and society to float; in individualistic conceptions it will, if consistently applied, result in anarchism; in the so-called trans-personalistic conceptions it will result in state absolutism. If the ideal of personality expands the boundaries of its rule still more, science itself will be in dire jeopardy, as Romanticism can teach us.

CHAPTER 2

ANTINOMIES IN HUMANISTIC LEGAL SCIENCE

Thus far we have taken note of the basic structure of the humanistic law-idea in its two antithetical well-springs: the sovereignty of personality and the sovereignty of reason. We shall now analyze a few of the many antinomies in which various elaborations of this law-idea has ensnared legal science and legal philosophy.

2.1 *Naturalistic types*

We will not now discuss those antinomies which the older rationalistic theory of natural law in its mathematical form had introduced to the field of the science of law. That theory is now said to be outdated and there is hardly any modern legal philosopher who will not begin his expositions with an unequivocal rejection of this obsolete rationalism. The method of the science of law and that of legal philosophy has indeed changed. Immanuel Kant did not point to the limits of theoretical thought in vain. Nowadays, virtually everybody wants to be a positivist. Modern philosophy of culture, too, does not, in the field of law, dare to engage in constructions of natural law apart from the experience of positive law.

That said, we find the science of law—just to remain on the most positive ground—in a state of crisis, of chaotic confusion. There is a seemingly endless controversy about even the most elementary basics, about object and method. Since the days of Julius Hermann von Kirchmann's well-known address, *Die Werthlosigkeit der Jurisprudenz als Wissenschaft* [The Worthlessness of Jurisprudence as a Science], which jarred the conscience of students of the science of law, the bitter contest for control of the field has not subsided.

Remark: Kirchmann's published address appeared in the stormy revolutionary year 1848 and it entirely breathes the spirit of the then reigning natural-scientific positivism. The science concept of this humanistic school knew only eternal, immutable laws. With regard to the undeniable variable and temporal character of legal norms Kirchmann simply side-stepped the antinomy entailed in expanding natural scientific thought to the domain of law by denying the science of law the character of a science. In his address, exhibiting a most superficial spirit, found many protagonists and antagonists, demonstrating to what extent the modern, largely positivistically oriented theory of law was embarrassed by Kirchmann's attack. Notorious was his statement that "three emendations from the legislator have turned entire libraries into nonsense" (p. 17). Among the writings of the older critical scholars we mention: Friedrich Julius Stahl, *Rechtswissenschaft oder Volksbewusztsein* (1848), a work that leaves aside the scientific problem and focuses exclusively on opposing the practical political postulates of Kirchmann. Stahl correctly qualifies these postulates as conflicting with positive law itself. We should also mention the anonymous publication of A. F. Rudorff, *Kritik der Schrift des Staatsanwalts Von Kirchmann über die Werthlosigkeit der Jurisprudenz als Wissenschaft* (1848), as well as the work of C. H. L. Retslag, *Apologie der Jurisprudenz* (1848).

In modern times, in line with the critique of Kirchmann, the scientific character of the discipline of law is denied outright by writers like Max Rumpf, *Volk und Recht* (1910). On the basis of the monopoly of the value-free concept of theoretical science, only the natural sciences are appreciated as "sciences" or academic, scholarly disciplines; the discipline of history is called a "partial science" and the science of law a "non-science." Furthermore, for Arthur Nuszbaum, in an article in the *Zeitschrift für Sozialwissenschaft* (1906), the theory of law is only accepted as a "technique," merely in the service of jurisprudential practice.

A much more penetrating philosophical treatment of the problem is given by the neo-Kantian scholar Max Salomon in his work *Grundlegung zur Rechtsphilosophie* (1920). Salomon acknowledges Kirchmann's criticism to be correct; he opposes every attempt at locating the object of the science of law in legal norms which are necessarily arbitrary, variable, and often contradictory of the logical principle of identity (*sic*). Solomon believes instead that we can maintain the discipline of law as a science of *legal problems*.

On Solomon's work, see Julius Binder's article, "Der Wissenschaftscharakter der Rechtswissenschaft," *Kant-Studien* (1921). See also Binder's *Rechtsphilosophie* (1925), pp. 36ff.

In connection with this whole problem, see Theo Sternberg, *J. H. v. Kirchmann und seine Kritik der Rechtswissenschaft* (1908), pp. 12–35; Ernst Landsberg, *Geschichte der Deutschen Rechtswissenschaft*, 3 vols. (1880–1910), III/2, 735ff., and Hermann Marx, *Der Wissenschaftscharakter der Jurisprudenz* (1919).

[End of the Remark]

Sociology in modern times has increasingly begun to base itself on mass psychology as an empirical analytical science.

Remark: Sociology as a scholarly discipline is still in the preliminary phase of investigating its boundaries and its substrate, which explains the large diversity of conceptions regarding the method and field of study of this science. In his *Gesellschaftslehre (*1923), pp. 6ff., Alfred Vierkandt, professor of sociology and philosophy at the University of Berlin, distinguishes in this noteworthy book no less than seven different meanings in which the word *sociology* is currently employed.

Following Troeltsch (*Weltwissenschaftliches Archiv*, VIII, 260ff.), two main schools can be distinguished in modern sociology: the encyclopedic school concerned with the philosophy of history, and the formal analytical school. The former reaches back to the thought of Auguste Comte and exhibits all the possible nuances from biological naturalism (Spencer, Schäffle, Lilienfeld, Espinas and others) up to modern phenomenology, as in Max Scheler, *Der Genius des Krieges* (1915) and *Krieg und Aufbau* (1916). Some of the best-known modern representatives of this school are Paul Barth, *Die Philosophie der Geschichte als Soziologie* (1922), and Franz Oppenheimer, *System der Soziologie* (1922), whose ideal is a sociology as "the synthetic, encyclopedic discipline of culture on the one hand and the science of history on the other." This school's ideal is to grasp mankind's culture and history in an encyclopedic way as an integral whole.

The second, younger school is much more modest in its formulation of the problem. Its founders are Georg Simmel in his work *Soziologie als Lehre von den Formen der Vergesellschaftung* (1910), and his *Philosophie des Geldes* (1900); Ferdinand Tönnies, *Gemeinschaft und Gesellschaft* (1886); Emil Durkheim, *Les formes élementaires de la vie religieuse – le systéme totémique en Australie* (1912). The volume *Die Methode der Soziologie* (1908) is a kind of handbook of this school that is in search of an independent field for sociology *vis-à-vis* the other social sciences, a field which it believes is found in the "social fact," of which the essence is conceived as consisting of the purely intrinsic relationships of individuals within a group. It views sociology as a formal science, as the theory of the characteristics of the social group, or as the "theory of interactions and its effects" (Vierkandt), or as a "theory of relationships" (von Wiese). Unlike the older schools, it focuses on the problem of analyzing social phenomena, in which group and mass psychology (provided with a foundation by Sighele and Lebon) mainly presented the inductive method of research.

Important in this regard is the research of modern American and British sociologists. I refer to E. A. Ross, *The Principles of Sociology* (1921), and William McDougall (formerly private lecturer in psychology at Oxford, but currently professor in psychology at Harvard), *The Group Mind: A Sketch of the Principles of Collective Psychology* (Cambridge, 1920), and several others. Vierkandt, likewise a representative of analytical sociology, adds, next to the empirical, inductive sociology, a philosophical sociology as "Wesenslehre der Gesellschaft" according to the phenomenological method.

[End of the Remark]

Modern sociology believes it has already discovered a good number of unassailable laws[1] and it claims the science of law for itself. Thus, the modern "Freirechtsschule" or Freedom School of jurisprudence is largely based on a sociology of this type. In a variety of ways it seeks to replace the scholastic "*Begriffsjurisprudenz*" with an "*Interessenjurisprudenz*" on the pattern of Jhering and Adickes. Its practitioners are Eugen Ehrlich, Alfred Bozi, Herman Kornfeld, and, partially, Bohdan Kistiakowski, Hermann Kantorowicz, Erich Jung, and many others.

Remark: Compare Ehrlich's still highly instructive work, *Grundlegung der Soziologie des Rechts* (1913). On p. 19

he writes: "*Die Soziologie des Rechts ist die wissenschaftli-che Lehre vom Rechte*" (The sociology of law is the scientific theory of law"). According to Ehrlich, the sociology of law is an inductive "factual science" (*Tatsachenwissen-schaft*). The so-called "decision norms" (*Entscheidungsnor-men*), for which he reserves, in opposition to the school of conceptual jurisprudence (*Begriffsjurisprudenz*), mere-ly a very modest place within the whole of legal norms, "derive immediately from the societal structures. . . . Whenever law-conformity appears in the phenomena of legal life, which sociology is to discover and describe, it can only be there as conditioned by the societal and economic make-up of society and it can only be recognized and described in connection with the total social and economic development of society (p. 384).

In this way the science of law as sociology turns into a causal science: "The first task of the sociology of law is to bring together and summarize what is shared by legal relationships in disregard of the positive laws that hold for them, and to investigate the differences *as to their causes and effects*" (p. 386; ital. added).

What is called "national jurisprudence" then has to make way, of course, for an international sociology of law. Ehrlich cites (pp. 389ff.) Austin, Erskine, Holland, and Salmond, even though they were actually formalistic precursors of the international sociology of law. Other than that, the method of researching "living law" is broad enough. Legal history, ethnography, political geography, psychometric studies in the line of the Fechner-Wundsche School, where, in following the example of Professor Helmut Ofner in Vienna, participants are subjected to jural-psychological experiments with respect to their "legal sensitivity"—all these gain Ehrlich's approval. The only problem is that Ehrlich apparently did not realize that when sociology continues to speak of *legal norms* it can do so only by virtue of the jural anticipations within the social law-sphere. This also shows that sociology itself can never replace the science of law proper: it must constantly invoke the jural sphere.

Ehrlich's concept of science mixes up everything. For that reason, in spite of the often correct and important insights into the organic coherence between the jural sphere and the spheres arranged around it, this author cannot be a reliable guide on the laborious road of juristic method—to which he has dedicated a separate, comprehensive study, *Die juristische Logik* (1925).

A stark example of the methodological confusion that various modern sociologists of law from the Free School of jurisprudence are guilty of, is found in the work of Alfred Bozi, *Lebendes Recht* (1915), where it is stated:

> Just as the relations of motion of celestial bodies are already given with there existence, their attraction and repulsion, with the existence of human beings their legal relations are given, without any cognition or the necessity of being prescribed from an intrinsic or extrinsic source. The jural constructions are therefore relational numbers (*sic*) for the mutual connections of individuals and groups,

and only insofar as these relational numbers were altered through changes in the individuals involved, regarding the conditions of their groups and their lives, the legal configurations came into being and passed away. The task to construe the path of legal development and thus to provide a mathematical foundation to law is in principle not meaningless; its practical solution only collapses in an infinite number and the multiplicity of the factors involved. But it is always so that in subjection to the law the organic development by itself portrayed for legal development the image of a curve. For of the forces of inheritance and adaptation the former acts in the direction of a straight line and the latter in a side-ways direction. The effect must be portrayed in a side-ways displacement, for in cultural states the capacity to persist is dominated by the tendency to adapt (pp. 18–19).

For those who have followed our analysis of the humanistic law-idea, it will not be difficult to recognize that our entire exposition thus far clearly illustrates the *continuity tendency* of the metaphysical humanistic science ideal. My only caution is that it holds only for a *naturalistic* and not an idealistic type. Kantorowicz and Kistiakowski are closer to the standpoint of Jellinek, who is oriented to the dualistic view of law found in the Baden School [of neo-Kantianism]. In his work *Rechtswissenschaft und Soziologie* (1911) Kantorowicz views the science of law in a dogmatic sense as a normative discipline. But next to it he defines the history and sociology of law as cultural sciences in the sense of Rickert [thus as *individualizing* disciplines]. Like Radbruch and Jellinek,

Kantorowicz adheres to a position of value relativism.

[End of Remark]

In what is called "*ethnologische jurisprudenz*," ethnology has slipped its object into the science of law in order to uphold its scientific character against the fierce critique of Kirchman (A. H. Post, B. W. Leist, Franz Bernhöft, et al.).[2] The so-called neo-Hegelian School of Kohler has provided this method with something of a philosophical foundation. Psychology too, largely in alliance with modern sociology, has for a long time wanted to annex the science of law, whether in part or in its entirety (Theodor Lipps, August Sturm, Heinrich Bartsch, Franz Klein, Helmut Ofner, Wilhelm Schuppe, and, in part, Ernst Zitelmann and Georg Jellinek).[3]

These schools, which do not respect the boundaries between the jural sphere and those that surround it, have, each in their own way, imported an endless series of antinomies into the science of law, some of which will be summarized here by way of illustration. (Since the antinomies of the so-called natural schools have been sufficiently pointed out by Kelsen and his school[4] we do not consider it necessary to present any detailed analysis of them here.)

As to the confusion of boundaries between the science of law and psychology we may refer to the infamous dogma of the will or intention as crucial example, for it has been laid to rest so poorly in the theory that an epistemologically trained jurist of the largely anti-psychological Husserlian school has reintroduced it in all its glory, and in public appreciation of

Hobbes' theory of natural law.[5]

The antinomies in which this psychologistic dogma has embroiled legal theory are known all too well. Think only of the contradictions in the distinction between *"Rechtsge-schäft"* and *"Rechtshandlung"*; the contradictions in the problem of erring between mental reservation and simulation, etc.; the contradictions in the problem of the will of legal persons between *"furiosi"* and *"infantes"* [madmen and minors have no will]; in constitutional and international law, between the contradictory theories of a state's self-obligation and a state's voluntary self-restraint; in criminal law, the contradictory theory of a psychological cause of the will in an act of omission. At bottom, these antinomies all arose as a result of trying to derive normative legal consequences from a psychological concept of will. In the process, both psychology and jurisprudence suffered. Whenever psychical and jural givens are reduced to one denominator, in violation of the sphere sovereignty of their boundaries, it is clear in advance that there will be logical conflicts.

In the systematic theory of private law, the doctrine of the will or intention, as long as it remained current owing to Savigny's influence, was forced, despite its internal contradictions, to fit jural construction with the aid of fictions and restrictions. But wherever jural conscience no longer served as a brake on any consistent application of the dogma of the will, there its law-destroying character was immediately in evidence. Especially in the hands of politics based on natural law, it proved to be a most dangerous weapon. More than elsewhere else, this dogma has been most destructive in the area of international law.

It is characteristic of the peculiar tendency of continuity in humanistically oriented thought that it does not stop at blurring the boundaries between psychology and the science of law. Psychology in turn gets to be overgrown by physiology. Accordingly, Ernst Zitelmann, father of the modern "psychologistic" school in the science of law, described the will as "an act that works immediately upon the motor nerves and so becomes the cause of a personal bodily motion."[6]

When in addition the legal consequence too is seen as a causal effect of a declaration of will, then the naturalistic confusion of the boundaries between psychology, physiology, and the science of law is complete. Thus, Zitelmann defines a "*Rechtsgeschäft*" (legal action) as "the declaration of will directed towards the occurrence of a legal effect, which is the cause for the legal effect to occur."[7]

Remark: While Zitelmann still speaks of a causality *sui generis*, Wilhelm Schuppe even drops this reservation. In his work *Der Begriff des Rechts*, Schuppe qualifies law as the content of consciousness, as a *will*.[8] Its objective validity presumably is nothing but the category of "thing-hood" ("*der Dingheit*") to which both psychical and physical phenomena belong, and consists in nothing but "the unity to which a multiplicity of what is distinct coalesces through quite specific causal links." In order to escape from a psychological individualism Schuppe does not base law as a psychical phenomenon on consciousness of what is individual, but rather on the consciousness of *kind or class* (pp. 361–370). See also his

Grundzüge der Ethik und Rechtsphilosophie (1881).

Typical of Zitelmann's naturalistic method is also his view of a *subjective right*:

> But this is not sufficient, for now we also apply to this conceived thing [i.e., a subjective right] all those other forms of thought which we use for the world of the senses. Law is integral and divided, it is independent and dependent, it is one and many. We think of it as enduring (identical) notwithstanding the alteration of its properties (hence, for example, the concept of succession in law). What is most important, finally, is that we understand these rights, conceived as individual concrete entities, in the same way as we understand bodies: namely, with the aid of the category of *causality*. Just as the sensory world would immediately collapse into a disorderly mass of whirling atoms if the category of causality were no longer applied, so the legal order would utterly become a *rudis indigestaque moles* ["a rough and unprocessed heap"] if the application of the causal law were not transferred to it as well. But now we imagine these rights as coming into being, ceasing to be, and changing, like natural bodies. And for every such change in the world of subjective rights (the jural world) we must likewise find a cause similar to causes for changes in the surrounding physical and psychical world. In short, with all these mental operations we simply create a second world in the image of the natural world [*sic*]. We ourselves create the elements of which it consists, and then we connect these elements with each other. While these elements are merely something thought of, so also their connections are merely thought of. But within this once created mind-

scape, by virtue of our human authoritative word, they have the same position and worth as in the real world. Law is concerned with "copying nature into elements of thought." [9]

[The last words are from Jhering, *Jahrbücher* I, 12.]

[End of Remark]

And so the road leads directly from the psychological declaration of the will to the naturalistic causal concept of the will, from which even the psychologically essential moment of consciousness has been eliminated (cf. Karl Binding). Thus is born a new set of antinomies, in both the area of psychology and the science of law, as Christoph Sigwart has already demonstrated. Within the jural field of view, the causal concept of the will gives rise above all to the antinomy of a causality of omission, clearly a contradiction in terms, as well as the antinomy that the infinite series of causally determined consequences of an act of will must be jurally imputed—an absurdity that is supposedly barred by arbitrarily restricting the causal series in a way that would be unwarranted in natural science.

This whole confusion of methodologies and their inevitable antinomies need not be viewed as too great a tragedy. So long as it is confined to the area of theory, a well-developed jural intuition will find a way out of the labyrinth in which the blurring of boundaries has led the science of law.

The confusion appears to be less innocuous, however, when practical inferences are drawn from these theoretical errors.

Surely, it must be considered a serious infringement by psychology upon the field of legal science when Zitelmann wants to leave it to the psychiatrist to decide whether there is a case of insanity—a form of mental disturbance no less, to which jurisprudence has attached far-reaching legal consequences. Similarly, it represents a dangerous breach of the sovereignty of the jural sphere in general that whenever positive law employs a so-called "concept of life" without further defining it, Zitelmann as it were considers each science to whose area such a concept belongs to be fully authorized *ex professo* to give such a concept a content of its own choosing.

It gives one pause when Zitelmann begins to speak of a "natural law" in connection with such infractions against the sovereignty of the science of law. He writes: "These relationships, which by nature remain unchanged, can provide the stuff of a *law of nature* that would have a more secure existence than what is currently known by that name." This can only mean the usurpation of the jural area by natural science.[13] One need think only of a criminal law concept like "accountability" or "not criminally responsible" to become aware of the very serious practical danger of Zitelmann's psychologism.

The violation of the boundaries between the various areas becomes extremely dangerous indeed when it takes place knowingly at the prompting of humanism's meta-physical ideal of science; when, in other words, the humanistic world and life view in its naturalistic type begins to import its dangerous political tendencies into science. This danger is imminent for the science of law, especially from the quarters of

modern sociology. Ever since Comte worked out the humanistic ideal of science into a "positive" philosophy that considered all phenomena as phenomena of immutable laws of nature that should be reduced to the smallest number possible,
sociology was proclaimed a natural science encompassing all
areas of human society. The concept of science, the mathematical natural scientific method of Galileo and Descartes,
was posited as an explicitly metaphysical ideal of science in
service of humanity, of culture, of the human being: "The
good of humanity is the ultimate criterion! It is from science
that we expect it," wrote Comte, while a modern author of
the sociological school of Ernest Solvay expressed the essentially personalistic ideal of science in the following enthusiastic way: "It is from it [science] alone that we must demand
clarification and guidance, so that we will wish, through
progress, to advance the march of society towards a superior
state of humanity."[14]

The science ideal of continuity metaphysics has here embodied itself in a type of the humanistic law-idea that postulates the unity of all laws in the unity of a universal law of
nature which encompasses the entire cosmos.

Gustav Ratzenhofer, author of the famous work *Wesen
und Zweck der Politik* (1893), who thought he had established sociology and politics on a purely positive-scientific
basis, discovered subsequently that his positivistic method
was based on a philosophical foundation. That basis was a
rationalistic humanistic law-idea which he called the basic
law of "*der Urkraft und das inhärentes Interesses*": primal force
and inherent interest. All phenomena, natural and cultur-

al, were but a differentiation and integration of this *Urkraft* which, continuously operative, bridges and levels all boundaries of law.[15] In the light of this law-idea, the state becomes the product of the clash between different social groupings, among which arises—depending on their nature—adjustment, or compromise, or social struggle. The latter leads to a relationship of domination that is the essence of the state. The functions of the state are: the protection of morals as the product of adjustment; protection of the common law as the product of compromise; and determination of positive law as the "effect of the social struggle."[16]

A fresh stimulus went out from modern energetic natural science, founded by Robert Mayer. It proposed to establish methodologically the logical continuity of all the sciences. Ernest Solvay, founder of the well-known Institutes by that name, wished to base sociology as a science on the physical-chemical laws of the conservation of energy, the equivalence of energy transformations, the law of entropy and the principle of "*travail maximum*" (maximal performance) which, as universal laws of nature, govern all phenomena, including those in the fields of psychology, law, and ethics.

> **Remark:** Cf. writings by Solvay: *Science contre religion* (1879); *Industrie et Science* (1910); *Le productivisme social: Questions d'Energétique sociale (*1894–1910); *Notes sur le Productivisme et le Comptabilisme* (1900*);* "Sur les Fondements positifs bio-psychiques et énergéto-productivistes de l'évolution sociale," *Revue économique internationale* 10 (Dec. 1913); *Principes de politique sociale (Questions d'énergetique sociale)*; *La Théorie des*

échanges et la Notion du productivisme sociale; and more.

Solvay and his disciples introduced the following general principles of modern energetic natural science as universal principles for the fields of sociology and politics: the conservation of energy, the equivalence of energy transformations, the degradation of energy (entropy), and the principle that "every chemical change occurring without the mediation of foreign energy has the tendency to release a maximum of productivity." (Berthelot, who discovered the latter, spoke in a less precise way of a "maximum of caloric energy.")

In this way an attempt was made to subsume social development under the general energetic law of entropy. Typical is this statement by Solvay:

> It is therefore uniquely under the sway of energetically determined tendencies that mankind managed to gain control over the physical and chemical elements which constitute its environment. Mankind today controls the environment to which beings of a lower order are enslaved, and there is evidence that in the end all its actions combine *to utilize and degrade the natural energies step by step*, which can only end in a considerable enlargement of the power which mankind possesses and which lower animals use organically in their self-degradation of energy. Yet man is always obliged by his intelligence to act in this way: he submits, as by law and in his own interest, to the necessity of multiplying the degrading actions of his own organism. (*Industrie et science*, pp. 13–14, ital. added)

At this point, of course, a *metabasis eis allo genos* (category mistake) is already made: a change from a natural law to a norm. Cf. Barnich, *Essai de politique positive*, p. 135: "Having completed the energizing theory of Solvay, envisaged from the viewpoints of individual and society, these allow us henceforth to formulate the synthesis *not only of society as it is, but also of that which it must be if it is to stay true to the laws of nature.*" (ital. added)

[End of Remark]

Wilhelm Ostwald wrote in the same vein in his *Energetische Grundlagen der Kulturwissenschaft* (1907), where he degrades law to a regulator of social energy consumption, while stigmatizing the customary words '*penalty*' and '*punishment*' as reminders of the derivation of law from the relationship of slavery, a culturally hostile atavism.[17]

Ferdinand Tönnies too considers the natural-scientific concept of energy to be the logical bridge which via psychology joins human culture to nature. He writes: "Hobbes is a materialist in the sense in which the whole world is so, or more and more becomes so." And he continues:

It is of course a big and difficult leap that separates him [Hobbes] from Spinoza. Despite many attempts, contemporary biology and psychology shrink back from taking this step, for only their tendencies lead to rational consequences. But this step is not, as a superficial view sees it, the step from natural science to *metaphysics* (in its usual sense). Like Hobbes and the positivist natural scientists, Spinoza aims at a description and explanation of the facts of experience in a way that is as perfect as possible. It is the fear of new and unfamiliar *concepts* and a lack of clarity about what *can be known at all* that men are resigned with false modesty to continue to plead ignorance. . . . But if that concept of being or substance were understood properly, it would once again coincide with that of "energy," a concept which is equally neutral vis-à-vis the "attributes" of body and spirit, yet as a rule cannot resist being conceived and understood as material, and, when needed, as psychic.[18]

The antinomies that result from a serious attempt to apply the ideal of science in this way find only an apparent solution in the total destruction of the concept of law, an abrogation of the science of law and a reduction of all norms to laws of nature; it is an attempt which naturalism cannot carry out consistently, if only because it would have to deny its political tendencies in doing so.

Hence, the antinomies between modern sociological legal theory and the boundaries which hold good for the jural sphere continue to exist in undiminished strength.

Ratzenhofer, for example, explains the rise of societal life from differentiation of the *Urkraft* (primal force): the individuals (plus the social groups they enter) strive for that metabolism which is most beneficial for their development in view of their inherent interest, and they attempt to repel and destroy anything in the social struggle that might block their adjustment. Hence Ratzenhofer regards the entire societal order, including the state, as a result of mutually inimical forces. Clearly, this entire conception is marked by a lasting antinomy between justice and power, between norm and natural force. The moment this conception enters the science of law, an endless series of antinomies necessarily crops up between inherently jural categories such as authority, duty, accountability, guilt, punishment, and so on, and naturalistic categories like that of cause and effect, adjustment and non-adjustment, power and struggle, and so forth. In a case like that, it would be more honest no longer to speak of the science of law, but instead of a natural science of societal life, as it is done by Gumplowic.[19]

Nevertheless we see how the modern sociological school—save for a few radical exceptions like Kraepelin[20] and Thomsen[21]—continues to hold fast to the concepts of punishment, guilt, accountability and *"Tatbestand"* (the facts of the case)—although the necessary determination of psychical life by the social milieu is maintained most emphatically over against the postulate of moral freedom, and although punishment is denatured so as to be a mere protective measure against future social behavior.

Punishment must be directed, not at the deed, but at the anti-social attitude as determined by the social environment. On these matters Professor von Overbeek observes correctly that there is an unresolved antinomy in the concepts of the modern school: in view of their sociological starting-point, concepts like facts, attempts, participation, and coincidence, and concepts like punishment and guilt as well, must lose all meaning.[22]

Therefore, it is perfectly logical that the well-known Italian draft-legislation for the revision of penal law (Part, I, 1921), in which the basic ideas of the leader of the Italian school, Enrico Ferri, are consistently applied, omits the jural concepts of guilt and punishment. It speaks of *responsabileta legale* (responsibility before the law) instead of "guilt," and of sanzione (sanction) in the place of "punishment" (see Sanction V). The rational and jural justification of coercion against individuals who undermine the foundations of social life is sought in the inevitable natural law of social adjustment.[23]

But, we might ask: why does this school continue to speak of "*Tatbestand*" as necessary condition for the introduction of pseudo-criminal legal sanction?

This inconsistency is defended in terms of basically two considerations, the first of which is simply untenable, while the second in a most surprising way highlights the fundamental antinomy between the science-ideal and the personality-ideal in the humanistic law-idea.

The first argument is that of the symptomatic significance of the offense. Only the deed can justify the conclusion that the social danger, the anti-social attitude, was indeed present in the delinquent. As if, in the deterministic fashion of the sociological school, the hazards of the social environment (poverty, poor housing, etc.) and the totality of all social behavior ought not to be symptoms that are equally certain!

The real reason, however, is implicit in the second argument. It is the interest of personal freedom which opposes abandoning the individual (without guarantee of legal security) to the general interest of civil society! It is the final, desperate, resistance by the personality-ideal against the tyrannical domination of the science ideal! A resistance, which, unjustified in view of the scientific starting-point, clearly demonstrates at once the antinomy inherent in this naturalistic law-idea.

2.2 *Idealist-functionalist types: the Marburg School in neo-Kantian legal theory*

We shall now leave this summary of a few of the most prominent antinomies in the naturalistic schools, to focus our attention on a second type of humanistic legal theory with its inherent antinomies. This theory is strongly opposed to naturalism. By constructing a "*Reine Rechtslehre*" (pure legal theory) on epistemological foundations, it seeks to purge legal science of naturalistic admixtures.

We have in mind the neo-Kantian school of positivistic legal theory oriented to the so-called Marburg School of Hermann Cohen, Paul Natorp, and Ernst Cassirer. Since I have recently subjected the conceptions of the Marburg School to a critical analysis in the *Tijdschrift voor Wijsbegeerte*,[1] let it be enough here to indicate in broad outline the general spiritual direction of these neo-Kantians.

The Marburgers form a school of philosophy that proceeds from Kant, but unlike Kant's static transcendental logic, which unites thought and intuition, they give prominence to the dynamic and creative nature of thought, reject the value of intuition for knowledge, and recognize for the whole area of "*die reine Vernunft*" (pure reason) only the sovereignty of creative thought. Being and thinking become identical. The *Gegenstand* is created by thought alone. "*Die Erzeugung selbst ist das Erzeugnis*": the product itself is the production" (Cohen). Instead of Kant's restriction of the categories of reason to intuition, they accept Leibniz's idea of the creative continuity of thought[2] as well as his concept of function, purged of the metaphysical admixtures of an operative force. In view of the logical origin, the logical basic relation of thought, they posit that all categories must spring forth from this origin in strict continuity. The *Gegenstand* is to be brought ever closer to its determination by dint of the infinite creative activity of thought. Essentially it is the logic of infinitesimal calculus that makes its entry here and obeys the fundamental law of continuity in differentiation and integration. The category becomes a functional method of thought, not a static essence as in Kant, and it continually refers back to the origin and forwards to new categories that are generated in the restless dialectical movement of thought. In all this the Marburg School shows a clear attraction to Hegel's philosophy of identity, even though it rejects the primacy of the ideal of personality.

For orientation on this adventuresome road of the creation of the *Gegenstand* from the logical origin, the "*Faktum*" (or, rather, "the *fieri*," the practice) of science must do duty. Theoretical thought is to use the "*fieri*" of mathematical natural science as its compass. Starting from the *Logik der Reinen Erkenntnis* (the logic of pure knowledge), the *Grundsatz der Wahrheit* (axiom of truth) leads thought itself to the *Ethik des reinen Willens* (the ethics of pure will), which likewise is to proceed, in a creative way, to generate the *Gegenstand* of ethics, pure will, from its origin in its continuous unfolding in act, law and self-consciousness (Cohen).

Remark: Cohen rejects Kant's "primacy of the practical reason." Cf. *Ethik des reinen Willens* (1921):

> Ethics is not served by such a privileged value. If an over-emphasis on moral feeling plays logic off against ethics, religious morality may triumph over it, but ethics and ethical truth are not advanced by it. Ultimately, religion too is not served by what is excessive. . . . (p. 90)
>
> Truth, as it should be conceived by ethics, must be the truth of knowledge. Knowledge, however, is in the first place logic. And ethics must not deviate or depart from this logic. . . . Truth without the presupposition of logic is inadmissible. For all that, logic, by itself, has correctness, law-conformity, and universality, and necessity, but not truth. It is ethics that adds truth; but it brings it along. Ethics cannot obtain truth in isolation; it cannot create truth from within itself, for it is only in combination with logic that ethics grows towards truth. The last expression it not precise. Ethics does not grow towards the truth by connecting to logic and as it were mixing with it, since both types, and interests of reason generates truth as a new hallmark of knowledge and as the inner bond that keeps them together. (p. 89)
>
> . . . Truth means the coherence and harmony of the theoretical and ethical problem. This postulate must precede every construction of ethics. Therefore we designate it as the fundamental proposition of truth. (p. 91)

Cohen then postulates "*Einheitlichkeit*" (uniformity). See the very characteristic explanation on pp. 93–94 where the science ideal and the personality ideal are reconciled in a logicistic manner. See furthermore in particular the place where he treats continuity being carried through within ethics:

> Continuity [by contrast] must allow for being transposed to the will itself, if indeed this will, in accordance with continuity, is to be generated from its origin and thereby made into a pure will. Here therefore the danger arises that the full-blown mathematical continuity may fall into dislike, when this concept is misused for ethics as a historical metaphor. . . . The *method of purity, on the basis of truth, demands conforming to the strict sense of continuity.* (105)[3]

[End of Remark]

In strict analogy with logical thought, ethics is elevated to become the logic of the humanities and is given the "*Fieri der Rechtswissenschaft*" (the practice of legal science) for a compass. The science of law becomes the mathematics of the humanities and lends its concepts to ethics.

Now then, this entire functionalistic method, in which we can easily recognize an extremely idealistic and rationalistic version of humanism's metaphysical ideal of science, has been applied to the science of law, though less by Rudolf Stammler than by the so-called normative school of Kelsen, including Kelsen's disloyal disciple, Fritz Sander.[4]

In essence, what is here imported into the science of law is modern functionalist-mathematical thought.

Ever since Kelsen, partly under the influence of Merkl and Sander, abandoned the static legal conception of his earlier works,[5] the Marburg concepts of "logical origin," "function" and "continuity" play a predominant role. The science of law, too, writes Kelsen, must fulfill the enduring task of all genuine science: namely, to determine its *Gegenstand* in a logically consistent system of pure concepts. Legal science must first of all purge its field of naturalistic elements; next, it must create a system of law in a necessary, continuous coherence of pure, functional concepts.

As the Marburgers banned the concept of "thing" or "entity" (the Aristotelian concept of substance) and replaced it everywhere with the thoroughly relative concept of function,[6] so Kelsen wanted to do the same for the science of law. Not only must the legal categories be robbed, in a functionalist manner, of their static character, but they must also be pried loose from all substrates that lie outside the area of law; and, furthermore, within the limits of this "*reine Rechtsdynamik*," (pure dynamics of law), the empirical legal phenomena must be ordered in a functional coherence.

Accordingly, I think one can detect a twofold dynamic in Kelsen's system: a purely transcendental dynamic among all pure legal categories (the dynamic of the *Rechtssatz*), and an empirical legal dynamic in the logical creation of the system of positive legal norms (the dynamic "*Erzeugungs-system der Rechtssätze*" (i.e, "the system that generates the legal propositions). This distinction roughly parallels Kelsen's distinction between, on the one hand, "Rechts*wesens-*" or "Rechts*formen*lehre" (i.e., a theory of the essence or forms of law, which focuses only on norms and their relations while abstracting their specific content), and on the other hand "Rechts*inhalts*lehre" (i.e., a theory of the content of law and . . .)—which in turn parallels Sander's distinction between a "*reines-*" and an "*empirisches* Rechtsverfahren" (i.e., a pure and an empirical legal procedure).

As far as the first point is concerned (the dynamics of the *Rechtssatz*), Kelsen lets the *Rechtssatz* play the part of logical origin in the sense of the Marburgers, in its function as pure form of thought, and then he has all other legal categories spring from forth from it in the judgments of the so-called "*Normlogik.*" In this logical sense the legal proposition (*Rechtssatz*), unlike all other judgments, is a hypothetical judgment in which two factual states of affairs ("*Tatbestande*"), the one as condition and the other as consequence, are joined together by the category of ought-to-be (*Sollen*). Expressed in a formula: "If a, then b ought to be" ("Wenn a, so *soll* b"), in contradistinction to the formula for a law of nature: "If a, then b also" ("Wenn a, so *ist* b").

Since law, in this sense, has a normative character, it is separated from all laws of nature by an unbridgeable gulf. Here, *Sollen* and *Sein* are two absolutely unrelated directions of thought: there is no bridge leading from the one kind of reflection to the other.[7] The *Rechtssatz* differs from the autonomous ethical norm, according to Kelsen, by its heteronomous and hypothetically coercive nature—by attaching execution or punishment, as a legal consequence, to human behavior as set forth in the first part of the hypothetical judgment as the condition for this legal consequence. The *Rechts-satz* does not distinguish itself from the norm of convention by its heteronomous character but by its normative character of coercion.

It would seem that this view makes a clean break with all kinds of naturalistic conceptions of law. Law is qualified by the hypothetical-normative form of judgment and is not generated except in the judgment of transcendental logic. It is not an imperative in the form of a "thou shalt," it has no addressee,[8] it expresses no will or intention in a psychological sense, and it is a purely objective-theoretical *Sollen* in a hypothetical form that differs totally from all the *Sein* judgments of natural science. The entire legal system consists exclusively of legal norms of this kind, and every legal norm must reflect the nature of all law if it is indeed to be a legal norm.[9] In the line of Paul Laband, Carl von Gerber, and Hugo Preusz, all teleological elements are kept out of the *Rechtssatz*. The end or goal lies beyond the legal concept[10] and is identical with the content of the law.

One might well call this statement of the *Rechtssatz* the statement of the logical origin of all legal categories. Let us examine this dynamic of categories more closely for a moment. First of all, the *Sollen* of the *Rechtssatz* appears in Kelsen to be identical with jural imputation. Of the two *Tatbestände* that are joined by the *Sollen*, at least the second, containing the legal consequence, has human behavior as its content. In a civilized state such a legal consequence (read: punishment) is attached only to a human action (of commission or omission); in primitive states, however, a certain punishment, say human sacrifice, is by no means unusual at the occurrence of a purely natural phenomenon (for instance, to avert the anger of the gods).

Also in cases like that, Kelsen the legal theorist wants to continue to speak of punishment and imputation. Thus, in his theory, imputation simply evaporates into nothing but an empty norm-logical relation between two *Tatbestände* which has precisely the same function as was just now attributed to the *Sollen* category itself. In other words, the "ought" itself is relativized, has become a normative relation, as such identical with the imputation but utterly separated from natural-scientific causality.

Kelsen will readily admit that this concept of imputation differs fundamentally from the current one in criminal law theory. But imputation in the latter sense is nothing but an ethical-political postulate, namely, the requirement that imputation will only take place where there is culpable behavior. This is simply natural law, and though Kelsen by no means rejects it in the political sense, in his "*Reine Rechtslehre*" it is contraband.[11]

Where imputation in the sense of imputing to the human person(ality) has thus been eliminated, it need not surprise us to find that the categories of legal subject, legal obligation, subjective right, lawfulness, unlawfulness, government and subject in their specifically static sense disappear as well. All of them become functions of the *Rechtssatz*. They are the *Rechtssatz* itself, in a variety of functions.

In line with the logic of the Marburgers, the legal subject or legal person becomes a mere "starting point for relations," a personification[12] of norms, applicable equally to a contract, a partnership, and an association. It is a geometrical point of intersecting lines of imputation to a norm-system or a part thereof.

Here the category of imputation reveals its second function. In the category of person a *Tatbestand* is imputed to the unity of the legal order or a part thereof. Here imputation is central, whereas in its earlier function of formally connecting two *Tatbestände* within the legal norm it had only a peripheral character (*Allgemeine Staatslehre*, p. 65). The state as legal person is but the legal order as a united whole. Legal order and state are identical. The jural will or intention is nothing but the "*sollen*" or imputation category. The will of the state is the legal order itself and all particular norms are imputed to it. Every distinction between government and subjects, therefore, has disappeared. The only government is the legal order itself. To this legal order everyone is equally subject. At least in this respect Kelsen fully agrees with Hugo Krabbe and Léon Duguit. Also eliminated is subjective right as a substantial independent category. Kelsen is emphatically opposed to the idea of an independent subjective right distinct from an objective right such as maintained in Jhering's theory of "*rechtlich geschütztes Durchschnitsinteresse*" (legally protected average interest) or as defended in the theory of will-power, since he suspects (and rightly so) that these theories form a hotbed of natural law, while, as a faithful disciple of Bergbohm, he has sworn to reject natural law, at least in theory.

As an alternative, Kelsen advances his conception of subjective right as a mere function of the objective norm. It is nothing but a delegation by one or more persons for the determination of justice in an individual case, an authorization by the objective legal order to provide general abstract legal norms with a more concrete, individual content (e.g., in a contract). Right and obligation, therefore, constitute an inseparable unity. No law without obligation.[13]

Legal obligation too becomes but a logical normative function. In Kelsen's sense, legal obligation is simply the legal norm seen from the point of view of those whose behavior constitutes the content of the jural *Sollen*. In other words: legal obligation derives exclusively from the prescription of a legal consequence. No legal obligation without juridical sanction![14]

Injustice may no longer be viewed in a formal jural sense as an unethical (!) negation of law; rather, it must be incorporated within the dynamic system of law, where it will be nothing but a "condition of the act of coercion attached to it by legal judgment, the so-called result of injustice."[15]

Such, in skeletal form, is Kelsen's dynamic theory of legal categories.

Next, behind, or rather within, this problem of pure legal forms looms the problem of the content of law. Cohen, Natorp and Cassirer claim they can determine the very content of the Gegenstand "nature" in an infinite process of thought, creating it logically by means of the "*logic of pure knowledge.*" That is how concepts were created like the infinitesimally small, number, space, mechanical movement, and finally even the specific concept of energy in the natural sciences (as a logical constant in functional causality). Now then, in an analogous way Kelsen has ventured logically to create legal content, not, that is to say, in the sense that he wants to take over the creation of empirical law from legislator, administration, judge or custom, but only in the sense that he wants to indicate the method by which the science of law can create all empirical law in the continuous functional coherence of a logical system, thus finally turning law into a *system of knowledge.*

On this point Kelsen has largely accepted the theory of his disciple Adolf Merkl about the *"Stufenbau des Rechts"* (tiered structure of the law),[16] a theory that apparently tended to take the wind out of the sails of the modern Free Law movement. Like natural science, the science of law too must begin with a logical hypothesis and accept a so-called *norm of origin* which, as basic law, must logically underlie and support the entire legal system. In this norm of origin, the sovereignty of law, which is identical with positive law, is revealed to the extent that it expresses the absolute independence, the not otherwise deducible, nature of the legal order.

In this logical creative process, a new legal category presents itself, the formal category of the *legal organ.* The organ of the state as formal category is really nothing but the functional concept of the legal person in relation to the correlative creation or application of the state's will. It is the concept of the legal person as the personification of *Tatbestände* in the empirical legal dynamics.[17]

In the modern state the constitution must count as the primary concretization of the norm of origin. The constitution concretizes itself in legislation, legislation in ordinances and administrative measures, but also, and equally as much, in private law-making, as in contract law. Finally, the process from summons to sentence fits into the "*Stufenbau*" of law. The final concretization of law is the execution. In this way the entire system of law is created in a continuous process, the foundation of which, the norm of origin, does not as yet imply a compelling "*Tatbestand*," and whose final phase, the execution, is itself no longer a norm.[18] The system of law thus acquires a logical consistency, and cannot contain any flaws of logic. Objections to the dogma of the flawlessness of the law—advanced particularly by the notorious "*Begriffs-jurisprudenz*"—appear to be allayed since the monopoly of positive laws has been abandoned and all possible latitude for the concretization of law is given over to free discretion. However, all laws on a more concrete level must be traceable to the law of a higher "*Stufe*" or jural level.

Depending upon the political point of view that one accepts, the origin of the legal system may be placed in a state's constitutional law or in international law. To adopt the latter position is to reject the sovereignty of the state while all constitutional ordinances are seen as having been delegated by international law ultimately based on *pacta sunt servanda* as the "norm of origin." The advantage of this construction, apart from its ethical value, consists in the fact that the continuity of the state's order, even in case revolutions occur, can be logically understood, whereas to accord primacy or sovereignty to the state's order would make revolution jurally incomprehensible. To systematic legal theory, however, the two constructions are equivalent. This is the relativistic bent in Kelsen's theory!

Remark: Kelsen's most level-headed follower, Alfred Verdross, realized that Kelsen's standpoint on this issue, which again ends up surrendering the Pure Theory of Law to an ethical-political relativism, is untenable. Although Verdross initially held to the *primacy of constitutional law*,[19] he realized immediately the need for a monistic construction on a foundation of positive law.

In a later work, about laying the foundations of international law, Verdross abandoned his earlier standpoint and began to construct the unity of the legal system in such a way that international law, "at least in its leading issues," trumps constitutional law.[20] This standpoint he has worked out in a superb and compelling manner in a study of the unity of the legal world on the basis of international law,[21] a work in which he overcame so-called "positivism" by means of positivism itself. Much more seriously than his mentor Kelsen or Sander, both of whom dispose of the problem of the relation between constitutional and international law by delivering themselves of a few stereotypical formulas, Verdross offers a profound analysis of the two existing law systems in their reciprocal relationship, arriving at the conclusion that both Merkl's view of the primacy of constitutional law and Sanders' theory of the primacy of international law (which lacks all basis in positive law) are untenable.

For neither is the *entirety* of international law incorporated in the structure of national constitutions, nor is it layered over them. Rather, rising above constitutions are only those *Rechtssätze* which we have singled out as fundamentals of international law, while the rest of international law arises in the practice of judicial proceedings, which again depend on national constitutions. . . . In any case, national constitutions insert themselves between the entirety of international law and any *Rechtssätze* of international law.[22]

The "*Rechtssätze* of international law" meant here is the jural basis for every national constitutional sphere that stands in a relationship to international law—which nowadays can be said of every nation-state.[23] And then it turns out, following an analysis of existing international law, that it recognizes not just treaties and customs but alternately also *international justice, hence naked natural law itself,* as the legal source of international law, and that the norms of this international justice take on positive form in the science of international law, so that this science serves alternately as a source of law.

Thus, we experience the intriguing spectacle that in international law the web between contract law and customary law on the one hand, and justice on the other, which "unpositive" *positivism* must mark as a mistake of natural law and therefore must strive to expunge, was actually spun from the praxis of international law, i.e., from a specific level of law. But if it concerns *legal acts* that relate to justice, albeit merely as an alternate source of international law, then it conforms in no way to a genuine positivistic method that seeks to tear apart this law-conforming co-herence.[24]

If we understand this correctly, then Verdross has here not only vanquished "metaphysical" positivism, but also the "generating methodology" of the Marburg School, even though he formally continues to pay all possible respect to the School. For when he notes that "the construction based upon the 'dualism' between in-ternational and constitutional law is to be rejected, *not on methodological grounds*, as Kelsen holds, but because in the experience of legal judgments both legal domains are found to be bound to each other. . .",[25] then he essen-tially denies the sovereignty of *Normlogik*," the *logically creative* activity of the "pure theory of law."

The same applies also to that other pupil of Kelsen, Walter Henrich, who in his study of the theory of the territory of the state emphatically opposes his teacher re-garding the impossibility of dissolving political theory into jural epistemology.[26]

[End of Remark]

The type of antinomies in which this neo-Kantian legal theory must necessarily involve itself can be known in ad-vance. What we have here is an attempt to rescue the sov-ereignty of law by positing that it cannot be derived from a higher order of norms as against all other orderings, both natural and ethical. And this attempt is made by abstracting law as a pure form of thought and by creating positive law in the process of thought as a logically consistent system out of a *norm of origin* with the aid of the mathematical concept of function, similar to the way the logic of natural science is supposed to indicate the method by which to create the system of nature. It is the same urge for continuity of the humanistic science ideal as that which we found to be at work in the naturalistic types of humanistic legal theory. The only difference is that with Kelsen *cum suis* law is not first reduced to a natural thing (power, energy, or a causally malformed process of the will) but, instead, is formally and wholly severed from nature by the hypothetical *Soll*-form, even as the functionalistic method maintains continuity with natural scientific thought.

In this way, too, all conceptual boundaries fade away, albeit idealistically this time, yet no less than they did under naturalism in a materialist sense. The very first antinomy that must therefore show up is an unresolvable incongruity between the normative form, which is still reserved for law, and the so-called norm-logical method. When thought is declared to be sovereign, the legal order cannot simultaneously be maintained as a sovereign, not further reducible, order over against the claims of other systems of thought. Analysis therefore will bring to light that Kelsen's sovereignty of law indeed entails the destruction of the sovereign character of the legal order. Not law but mathematical logic will turn out to be the real sovereign. Once again, the basic antinomy in the humanistic law-idea—that between the ideal of science and the ideal of personality—will come to light. Furthermore, given the logical-mathematical woof and warp of the system, the supposedly positivistic nature of Kelsen's legal theory will turn out to be (to stay in the terminology of the school) "the mask of a naked natural law." A continuing antinomy between the true character of all positive law and the logical fundamentals underlying Kelsen's positivism will be revealed, while, finally, it will become apparent that law simply can not be approached in this way, but that instead thought is trapped in a vicious circle from which a bridge to the reality of law cannot be found.

The first of the antinomies predicted does indeed reveal itself in an appalling fashion in the so-called form-content problem.

In the footsteps of Immanuel Kant, *Sein* and *Sollen* are set side by side as two completely independent directions of consciousness. But it is forgotten—and this is a fatal misunderstanding of Kant's humanistic ideal of personality—that with the Koningsberg philosopher *Sollen* is not a category of the understanding but a regulative idea, so that in Kant the entire form-content problem loses its meaning in the areas of law and morality. Neither in Kant nor in Cohen[27] is *Sollen* a constitutive category, and cannot, at least in Kant, be focused on possible experience, as surely ought to happen if the so-called hypothetical *Sollen* were indeed, as Kelsen asserts, a form of thought for the determination of the content of law.

If, contrary to Kant, one does want to maintain the category of *Sollen* as a thought-form that determines all empirical law, then one must first demonstrate how it is possible that, on the one hand, reality without exception is subject to the universal validity of natural causality, while, on the other, reality can also be regulated by a system of norms that is perfectly heterogeneous with that causality. Kant himself, as we saw earlier, allowed the norm to obtain only as *idea*, and always opposed recognizing *Sollen* as a category of thought, a category of *science*.

An organically conceived law-idea, like that of Calvinism or Thomism, could break the impasse at this point, but the humanistic law-idea is, nominalistically, devoid of any organic character and stands helpless before the apparent antinomy between two law-spheres. In humanistic conceptions the law-spheres cannot but clash and demolish each other, and refuge can only be sought in the realm of the ephemeral ideas to save at least the nebulous, unreal, idea of sovereign personality.

In Kelsen, the antinomy indeed follows a tragic course of development. First, the category of *Sollen* is quickly dissolved into the category of imputation, and, given Kelsen's concept of imputation, into a mere logical relation. Now a relation, in and of itself, is unable to mark off a field of vision or angle of approach from another. *No relation can exist without a founding modality*, and by modality I understand (unlike critical philosophy) the *absolute, qualitative category in which the sphere sovereignty of any one law-sphere expresses itself as different from other law-spheres.* Thus, once the criterion between nature and right is sought in a mere relation, the entire distinction is relativized and, essentially, abolished.[28]

Consider for a moment what remains of the true character of the norm when it is hollowed out to the point of being a mere relation of imputation in which the subjective moments are reduced to *Tatbestände*, the norm-subject (the person) to a function, and a legal obligation to a logical relation. In this sense the imputation with all its subjective elements is in fact no longer distinguishable from functional causality as it appears in modern energetic natural science, where it ends up as a coordination of equivalent quanta of energy or as a relation of imputation as it is found in modern set theory—in the same way as one of Kelsen's disciples, Fritz Schreier, has denatured the concepts of law into relations of imputation in the sense of set theory.[29]

The inherent consequence of the humanistic ideal of science is perfectly illustrated in Kelsen's ex-disciple Sander. As is well known, Sander has most vehemently opposed Kelsen's normative school of law by analyzing the conception of law as a norm and characterizing it as a dogmatic ethical-political prejudice.[30] For Sander, the legal order is found within the spatially and temporally determined reality of *Sein*, not in the dimension of *Sollen*. That is indeed the consequence of Kelsen's functionalism. Sander nevertheless retains the categories of imputation, the *Tatbestand*, legal competence, and fault. But with him imputation is nothing but a functional attribution of all elements of the *Tatbestand*, not toward a subject, but toward each other.[31]

In the course of a *Rechtsverfahren* (legal action) the state is but the logical constant (modern natural science's "*Substanz-begriff*") Sander does not have law created logically by the science of law, as does Kelsen, but instead by an epistemological activity, namely by the application of "*Zurecht-Erken-*

ntnis" (knowledge of what is right) on the part of competent agencies (organs) of the legal order, who, in doing so, by no means pronounce judgments about what *ought to be*, but only pure judgments of what *is*, in the temporal modes of representation (*modo praesente, modo praeterito* and *modo futuro*).[32]

In this process of law-creation Sander sees a perfect analogy with the creation of nature in natural science. Nevertheless, he too wants to maintain law as a sovereign sphere, albeit as a sovereign sphere within the world of "is": of *Sein*, not *Sollen*. In his earlier, second phase, and stimulated by the Marburg School's functionalistic ideal of continuity, Sander was not much bothered by the question how law could be such a sovereign sphere in the world of *Sein* next to the causal sphere of nature. Law was to create itself dynamically by logical synthetic judgments "*des reinen Willens*" (of pure intention) in the legal process. In fact, it was in a detailed analogy with Kant's transcendental deduction of the categories of the intellect that Sander tried to deduce the categories of legal experience, an analogy that resulted in a complete identity with the categories of natural experience. Accordingly, he saw no problem at all in speaking of an *extensive* and an *intensive legal entity*, or of *legal substance* and *legal causality*. After some critical reflection, however, Sander had to come to the realization that in this way the sovereignty of the legal process could not be rescued, since there was no room in Kant's two-realm view for a sovereign *empirical jural sphere*.

In his third phase, Sander now tried to topple the Kantian dualistic theory as dogmatic. Taking his cue from Brentano's act-psychology and Husserl's phenomenology,[33] he gave a descriptive analysis of the acts of organs as *"Rechtsakte"* (legal acts) in their noetic and noematic aspects, from which it was to become clear that law has its own *"Gegenstandsregion"* with its own proper categories. The science of law would then remain purely reflexive as opposed to the constitutive legal process which sees the judgments of law as "is" judgments and not as "ought" judgments. In the legal process itself, meanwhile, the Marburger ideal of continuity prevailed in full force. This resulted in an impossible combination of two different philosophical systems—a situation similar, for that matter, to the fundamental error of the whole of phenomenological legal theory when it supposes that it can join Kelsen's functionalism (oriented to the Marburg School) to Husserl's static-eidetic method.

> **Remark**: Thus far, only Adolf Reinach, in his *Die apriorischen Grundlagen des bürgerlichen Rechtes* (1913), has attempted to provide a purely phenomenological analysis of legal consciousness on the basis the "social act"—without impairing his method by the interference of "norm-logical" elements from Kelsen's system. In so doing, he immediately got entangled in an antinomy between positive law and the "*a priori* propositions" of civil law analyzed by him (op. cit., p. 117). A veritable antinomy indeed, for how can positive law come into conflict with these "*a priori* foundations"? Reinach then aims at a solution to this problem by assigning to these *a priori* propositions the character of *judgments* about the essential and necessary "ontic coherences" while at the same

69

time measuring positive law against the "determinations" of the "ought-to-be" (*Sein-sollende*) in an attempt to defend the sovereign freedom of positive law vis-à-vis its "*a priori* foundations" (pp. 128ff.). But in so doing he actually determined the "essential laws" that he believed to have "discovered." (Compare Husserl's conception of the relation between "essential" and "factual sciences" in his *Ideen*, p. 18: "There is no [factual science] which, in its mature state, could be free of eidetic cognitions and so be independent from eidetic sciences, be they formal or material in nature.") Reinach's entire analysis negates the sovereign character of law, the perspective of the jural sphere.

One antinomy then follows upon another. According to Reinach, a promise made as a social act necessarily creates an obligation for the person who made it—indeed, a *moral* obligation. Is this also true of an immoral promise? Reinach indeed accepts this glaring antinomy. A promise to commit a murder or a theft creates, "essentially and necessarily," a *moral obligation*. This obligation is not based on the content but on the formal logical essence of the "promise." However, in order to escape the fatal consequences of this "essential law" in practice, the "moral" duty is then paralyzed by a still *higher* "moral" obligation (pp. 55 ff.). And so on, and so forth.

As for the other representatives of the phenomenological school of jurisprudence, they have largely come from Kelsen's school and now attempt—in vain, of course—to reconcile Kelsen's functionalism with the eidetic method of Husserl's phenomenology. Felix Kaufmann has attempted to achieve this goal in his above-mentioned work, *Logik und Rechtswissenschaft* (1922), as well as in his later study, *Die Kriterien des Rechts* (1924). See also his article, "Staatslehre als theoretische Wissenschaft" in *Kantstudien* 31.1 (1926).

Fritz Schreier has made a similar attempt in his article "Grundbegriffe und Grundformen des Rechts," *Wiener Staatswissenschaftliche Studien* 4 (1924). Typical for this entire school of thought is Schreier's statement:

> A jural norm is an *exact law*, not at the level of physical laws but *mathematical laws*. If synthetic judgments *a priori* are nothing but statements with the character of apodictic certainty, then we are fully justified in designating jural judgments as synthetical judgments a priori. A legal norm knows no exception and cannot be refuted by any new observations. Phenomena from the world of experience do not touch them at all. This constitutes their essential equality with mathematical laws and thus the words of Cohen acquire a new meaning: the science of law is the mathematics of the *Geisteswissenschaften* [humanities]. (Ibid., 33)

What we have demonstrated in the main text is here explicitly stated, namely that Kelsen's conception of *Sollen* as a logical relation of imputation ultimately denatures the concept of accountability and turns it into a relation of logical correlation in the sense of modern mathematical set theory:

We can therefore substitute the ought with the neutral term employed in mathematics, namely *Zuordnung* [correlation]. [The statement] *If a, then b* . . . , taken in a jural sense, states no more than that *b* (the legal effect) is correlated with *a* (the legal premise), and this once again leads back to the relation, for correlation is relation. The same applies to the concept of *Pflicht* (obligation), which we can put in the place of *Sollen*. Legal obligation, like legal *Sollen*, must be understood in a purely formal way, without taking any other meanings into consideration.

This line of thought leads in Schreir to the discovery of four basic concepts of law: facticity (*Tatbestand*), person, performance (*Leistung*), and sanction or penalty. The form of the legal judgment as a logical proposition (!) reads as follows: "When a *Tatbestand* or factual legal case is submitted, the Person ought to carry out the performance (*Leistung*) through the Sanction. These concepts are then designated by the letters T, P, L, and S.

> We do not introduce these alphabetic symbols as a playful analogy to mathematics, but in the first place to make sure we avoid every material conception, for the mere word *someone* can easily tempt a person to regard "someone" only as a human being. *Thus, we go back to the great design of Leibniz,* that of a "*caracteristique universelle,*" for which we want to make a contribution within the special area of law, even though in the present work it is not yet possible to fully carry through this idea of a sign language" (op. cit., p. 70; emph. added).

This shows with all the desired clarity that the trajectory of the humanistic science ideal is a combination of Leibniz' *mathesis universalis* with modern set theory in the form of a "pure theory of multiplicity" (in the sense of Husserl), above and beyond the continuity principle of Cohen's "pure logic." Schreier continues:

> The road chosen by the pure theory of law is the one already taken by mathematics in that it united itself with logic. Of course, this encompassing logic is no longer that of Aristotle: it is logic in the sense of the *scientia universalis* of Leibniz and of Husserl's pure theory of multiplicity." (p. 84) "The pure theory of law forms a part of the aim of all science, the *mathesis universalis*, and from this vantage point the connecting lines are to be drawn to other weighty disciplines which today of course are only in their initial stages, namely that of a formal axiology and a theory of praxis." (p. 85)

The "pure theory of law" now acquires the task to specify in an a priori manner the formal possibilities from which the legislator can choose. "With such a theory of jural possibilities, the pure theory of law presents itself as a jural theory of multiplicity" (p. 92).

[End of Remark]

Phenomenology, moreover, cannot help us here. At issue here is the delimitation of the natural jural field of vision within which Sander's "judgments of law" must operate, as distinct from other fields. Husserl, however, with the greatest clarity desirable, emphasized in his *Ideen* that phenomenology must begin with the "*Einklammerung*" (*epoche*) or bracketing of all angles of approach of all the sciences, natural and cultural, since these are founded in a natural posture of consciousness. In Husserl, furthermore, phenomenological reflection is unexpectedly accorded a *constitutive* character again, causing difficulty for Sander's distinction between a constitutive legal process and the reflexive science of law.[34]

In the end, Husserl's eidetics too takes place, basically, in a formal-logical framework that fails to do justice to the sovereignty of the jural. Since Sander appears to have noticed all these difficulties, he has recently made his fourth radical change of position in which the last vestiges of Marburg functionalism have been expelled and the revolutionary Sander has become a run-of-the-mill disciple of modern sociological legal theory (Max Weber's school) which he had opposed so vehemently before.[35]

That, as it were, is the dialectical process of the development of the antinomy in which the functionalistic conception of the relation between legal form and legal content must inescapably ensnare itself.

In Kelsen, the antinomy of the form-content problem reveals itself especially in the fact that the pretended absolute contrast between *Sein* and *Sollen* is logically self-destructive. Any arbitrary content can be attached beforehand to the functionalistically emptied "*Soll*"-form—his positivistic position takes pride in the attempt. Here we have the nominalistic destruction of the concept of norm which, in the end, serves merely to mask the crudest principle of will and power. The "norm of origin" of the legal system of absolute monarchy, for example, becomes: "Coercion must be applied under all the conditions which the monarch commands."[36]

Truly, this is the negation of all positive law, an inner contradiction on a par with the formulation of a law of nature in this form: "*Wenn a soll, musz notwendig b*" (If *a* ought to be, *b* must necessarily be).

In his treatment of the problem of legal positivity Kelsen in fact can no longer deny the antinomy produced by his humanistic ideal of science. Here the very thought which first posited an unbridgeable gulf between *is* and *ought* is compelled once again to place reality and norm in some relation to each other. Where sovereign thought refuses to bow to the divine laws of the jural sphere, logic itself is forced to try and construe the unmistakable coherence in which the various [cosmic] spheres of law relate to each other. At this point he makes a pitiful logical somersault. Mach's principle of the economy of thought is now called upon and expanded to serve the science of law as the principle of economy of values.

For the science of law this principle then stipulates that the tension between the scientifically construed legal order and the actual behavior of people subject to that order may never become so great that the legal norms would be entirely without effect. In other words, thought has already sacrificed the pretended logical sovereignty of law and has posited an internally contradictory *logical* relation between *is* and *ought*. Kelsen is quite correct when he observes: "The exceptional difficulty that it entails consists in the seemingly inescapable antinomy of having to presuppose a dualism of *Sein* and *Sol-*

len, of reality and value, and of being forced to acknowledge a material relation between the two—earlier presumed to be unrelated—systems."[37]

Meanwhile, we have still not penetrated to the heart of the antinomy in the form-content problem of Kelsen's legal theory. The deepest source of this contradiction lies in the fact that Kelsen equates content and purpose of the law. Already in his *Hauptprobleme* Kelsen held forth that legal concepts are but formal categories, and that the science of law need only deal with the "form of [legal] phenomena," the content of which is the concern of sociology and the historical-political sciences.[38] Where the purpose of law is transcendent to the law, there the content of law too must lie outside the law. To have effect, the law consists only of formal *Bedingungen* (conditions) and *Tatbestände* (factual findings), or, in other words, law is pure form. That would indeed be the consequence of Kelsen's premise, a consequence that would preclude any concept of positive law, a consequence therefore, that would amount to intellectual suicide for Kelsen the positivist. For, with that, the entire empirical dynamics with its "norm of origin" and *Erzeugungsmethoden* would have been placed beyond the limits of law and Kelsen's entire theory would shrivel up to become nothing but a mathematical theory of relations lacking a jural Gegenstand. The "norm of origin," after all, is by no means formal but consists of material natural law, and wholly lacks the hypothetical form of judgment that is specific to law. Kelsen's positivism therefore depends on a continuous contradiction of the basic premise.

The state is acknowledged to be a system of norms which,

if not exclusively, then at least in the main, have *human behavior* as its content. With that, space and time are likewise acknowledged as contributing content to legal norms. This immediately presents the problem of the relation between these norm-content elements and the jural form itself. If Kelsen were to be consistent, he would have to ban all these content elements from law as transcendent to the jural angle of approach. But Kelsen cannot remain consistent here. The entire Austrian school exists by virtue of this inconsistency. He must prefer to have the form of law accomplish a synthesis with the stuff of experience (which, he posits, belongs to the realm of nature), and so he embroils himself in the antinomy that law must take on a natural content that is controlled by the law of causality. He will gladly live with this antinomy to avoid that other one in which any consistent application of his norm-logical starting point would have bogged him down and which he himself candidly describes as follows: "If one were to reject space and time as [belonging to the] content of legal norms, if therefore one were to deny that the legal norm is valid somewhere and sometime . . . , it would mean that norms are valid nowhere and at no time; that is, they would not be valid at all. They would have no possible content, and, with that, no possible validity either.[39]

It should not be objected that Kelsen declares only legitimate human behavior (as the law's purpose) to be transcendent to the law,[40] while the content of the "factual conditions" and of the legal consequence can be considered "immanent in law" within the empirical *Rechtssatz*. For the content of the legal consequence can be nothing but legitimate human behavior: "Wenn *a*, so soll *b*." Even if, therefore, the obligation to behave lawfully has been eliminated from the "factual conditions," it immediately returns in the legal consequence.

Besides, from the "factual conditions" too, the obligation to behave lawfully has only apparently been removed. For here we find ourselves in yet another antinomy that Kelsen's *Normlogik* encounters as a result of the basic antinomy of the form-content problem, namely, the antinomy of the problem of injustice.

As we have argued when discussing the essence of antinomies, justice and injustice in their mutual relation may constitute a contrast but not an antinomy so long as one leaves the sovereignty of the jural sphere intact. Kelsen, however, has breached the sphere sovereignty of law for the sake of mathematical logic with its functionalistic law of continuity. Immediately, justice and injustice then relate to each other antinomously.

This antinomy has continued to be the constant crux of Kelsen's *Normlogik* and with sundry sophistic constructions he has endeavored to escape its clutches.

As long as he maintained the static point of view in which the legal person had at least some independence relative to the *Rechtssatz,* he had no problem ascribing injustice to private persons. The state alone, whose will is identical with positive law, could perpetrate no injustice.

However, the moment the legal subject was reduced to a mere function of the norm by a functionalist dynamic logic, the imputation of injustice became problematic everywhere. For consider: if legal persons are but personifications of legal norms, then how could they perpetrate injustice?

In his second major work, *Das Problem der Souveränität und die Theorie des Völkerrechts* (1920), Kelsen sought to escape the antinomy by the construction of a "secondary" legal norm in addition to the primary one, as well as by the construction of an "illegal" subject in addition to a legal subject. The latter two subjects could never be identical, for the same reason that Christian theology must place the person of God opposite that of the Devil. The state must be regarded as *the* legal subject, the point of imputation *kat' exochen* [par excellence] as the totality of the legal order. Other legal subjects, as personifications of parts of the legal order and points of imputation of human behavior, can only be construed on condition that other human actions are regarded as "compulsive acts," as "*gesollt*" and hence imputable. This is only possible by means of the hypothesis of a norm which requires sanction-avoiding (legitimate) behavior. This hypothesis, applied to the coercive order of the state, produces the *system of secondary legal norms* (*sic*) and the grouping of these norms from the point of view of individual economic and other kinds of interest, and provides the substrates for all the personifications created by legal subjects other than the state. The legal subject as personification of a complex of secondary legal norms, and, as such, the point of imputation for sanction-avoiding (legitimate) behavior, cannot simultaneously count as the subject of injustice, that is, of behavior that is a condition for the exercise of legal coercion.[41]

But this "solution," this dualistic pseudo-construction, could not but destroy Kelsen's postulate of continuity and constitutes a fatal blow to his "Pure Theory of Law."

In his third major work, *Der soziologische und der juristische Staatsbegriff* (1922), the dualistic construction has been abandoned again. Injustice is now merely a precondition for the exercise of coercion and as such has been incorporated into the legal system "conceived as law." Here as well, Kelsen does contrast legal subject and illegal subject, but where injustice has entered the legal system as *"Bedingung"* of the *"Staatsakt"* this dualism finally "urges on towards an ultimate unification."[42]

That is also the position which Kelsen holds in his latest major work *Allgemeine Staatslehre* (1925). Here the secondary legal norm is introduced as a "supporting hypothesis," according to which that which was first a single *Rechtssatz* now appears as the interrelation of several *Rechtssätze*. For example, when someone concludes a contract he ought to behave according to the norm of this contract; if he does not, however, then—at the request of the other party—he should be coerced to do so. Solely on account of this very specific legal consequence does the norm that prescribes the behavior agreed upon become a *legal* norm—a *relatively* independent, *secondary* legal norm. And a particular behavior is the content of a legal obligation only insofar as its contradictory opposite "is subject to the sanction of coercion, that is to say, is the condition for an act of coercion."[43]

Does that eliminate the antinomy? By no means. For the moment injustice is conceived to be part of the law, lawfulness and legal obligation become problematic as *concepts of legal content*. It amounts to a *hysteron proteron* (the order in reverse) when Kelson allows the legal obligation to be determined by the consequence of injustice. The norming of a legal effect can at most give rise to a legal obligation for the organs of the state, but never for the legal subjects. If, however, one joins Kelsen and denatures all legal categories into purely logical functions of imputation, then it is only confusing to continue to speak of norm, imputation, legal obligation, and legal subject. Then one might as well simply apply the logic of natural science, in perfect oblivion of the normative meaning of law. Precisely because Kelsen does not draw that inference from his *Norm-logik* but continues, with a tenacity incomprehensible to the superficial observer, to maintain *Sollen* und *Sein* as two completely disparate directions of consciousness—precisely because he wants both to continue to deal with law and at the same time to apply mathematical logic—therefore the antinomies of the form-content problem as we together have analyzed them above cannot but make their appearance.

Here already, we hit upon the inner basic antinomy of Kelsen's humanistic ideal of law. For his retention of the independent nature of the concept of norm derives from Kant's maintenance of the personality ideal over against the tyranny of continuity from the science ideal. But because the Marburg School assigned this very Sollen to the control, the sovereignty, of transcendental logic, it inevitably suffered degradation, to become a mere function of thought.

Allow me to point out a few other antinomies in Kelsen's "Pure Theory of Law." They bear out even more clearly our contention that his theory of legal sovereignty is indeed tan-

tamount to the annihilation of the sovereignty of law and
that it declares logical mathematical thought, rather than
law, to be sovereign. It shows up in the antinomy between
his critical positivism on the one hand, and the relation he
construes between law and the science of law on the other.
This once again highlights the fundamental antinomy between the ideal of personality and the ideal of science that is
found in every humanistic world and life view.

Kelsen is an avowed positivist and a sworn enemy of any
and all natural law. Even Stammler's natural law, with its flu-
id content and despite its degree of formality, is a fundamental error in the eyes of the Austrian school, which views it as
a relativization of the sovereignty of law for the sake of the
absolute norms of morality.[44] Meanwhile, Kelsen's "norm
of origin," as he himself candidly admits, is not positive law
but, rather, a logical hypothesis in the spirit of natural law.[45]
Positive law must find its sovereignty, its positivity, its normative source of validity outside of itself. Indeed, but where
does it find this source of validity? In the science of law, in
the mathematical method of sovereign thought. Fully in harmony with the Marburg School, Kelsen declares that law has
no other existence than as a "*Gegenstand der Erkenntnis*," as
an object of knowledge, a product of scientific thought. In
principle this thesis was always the basic dogma of all earlier
humanistic natural law, as Sander has rightly demonstrated,
notwithstanding the fact that the scientific method has since
moved into a critical phase!

Thus, the very postulate of the sovereignty of thought
drives positivism squarely into the arms of natural law, and

with that into an inescapable quandary. Whether this is a minimum content of natural law, as Kelsen states emphatically, is, to say the least, doubtful. If positive law is founded in a norm of natural law, its pith and marrow in one fell swoop likewise takes on the character of natural law. For, all the *Stufen* (levels) of the law ultimately depend on that natural law foundation. The entire legal order has become a product of natural law theory. Kelsen himself writes that the content of legislation, regulation, judicial settlement, etc. is not law *a priori*, but only *becomes* law by way of the hypothesis of law by which it is understood as law.[46] "*Recht ist was die Rechtswissenschaft als wahr erkennt.*"[47] That is: "Law is what the science of law recognizes as true." This single observation by Merkl characterizes the entire school. The fatal consequences of this fundamental antinomy can be traced to the very heart of jurisprudential theory. When it comes to the question of *legal force*, the crux of all logistic legal theory turns up in this appalling form, that for Kelsen and Merkl "the question whether nullity (in the legal sense) is present or not is a question of the logic of law," which in turn is decided "by the understanding of every evaluating *individual*, and not *in authoritarian fashion by the state.*"[48]

In Kelsen's legal theory, all positive legal precepts have the same value *a priori*, so that any positive legal flaw will *a priori* nullify an action by an organ of state as well. That is indeed the outcome of a logicistic theory, an outcome, we might add, that abolishes the legal order as such since it must be left to the choice of every individual intellect. After all, what is true for an action of the state applies *a priori* to laws, regulations, and contracts as well. In all cases where a legal norm, viewed from a higher level of law, exhibits a flaw in positive law, Kelsen's *Normlogik*, if consistent, has no choice but to consider it as a juristic "nothing." At this point, however, the theory shows an intolerable antinomy with positive law itself when it even ascribes legal force to ordinances and laws that have been promulgated in conflict with stipulations in existing law or in the constitution—provisional force of law in the case of ordinances, and even definitive in the case of laws, at least insofar as judicial review is withheld from the courts. Even so-called "void" juridical acts—think of nullification *ex tunc* (from the outset) and *ex nunc* (from now on)—certainly do have legal consequences. Legal nullity differs totally from logical nullity: it bears an undeniably teleological character.[49]

The normative school of the science of law is forced seek to extricate itself from this antinomy. It does so at the expense of encountering a new antinomy in the logical foundations of its own method. The intellectual father of this pseudo-solution is Kelsen's disciple Adolf Merkl.

Merkl retains the basic tenet that "every positive-law flaw in a legal norm or legal act will result in logical nullity, to be determined by the science of law." But an antidote to this severe logicism, he believes, is provided by the theory of the so-called "*Fehlerkalkül*" (error estimation). By this term Merkl means a stipulation in positive law that makes it legally possible to impute actions to the state which do not comply with all the conditions (determined by positive law) for its validity and that enables us to take such acts to be laws despite their juridical flaws.[50] Such a "*Fehlerkalkül*," however, can only be established by positive law, never by legal science. It is the embodiment in positive law of the political postulate that the legal order must reckon with the possibility that the application of its norms may not take place in a perfectly legitimate way because of errors of thought or a wrong intention on the part of its organs. In such instances positive law can allow such faulty acts to have the force of law regardless. In doing so it corrects itself, so to speak, by declaring its requirements for the validity of such acts, after the fact, to be mere wishes, which, if they are not met, very likely makes the organ accountable but does not make the action itself to be non-law.

The logicistic conception alone of the task of public administration and judgeship, evident in this entire conception, would, in and of itself, be offensive to every practicing jurist. It is not always errors of thought or a mistaken intention that often brings the law-enforcing organ in particular circumstances to the point of setting aside explicit legal stipulations. Justice and equity sometimes call for this.[51]

But even apart from this logicistic misconception, it can hardly be denied that Merkl's theory of "*Fehlerkalkül*" involves the so-called legal theory of *Normlogik* into new antinomies. Ater all, it now finds itself compelled, in order once again to avoid regarding non-law as law, to degrade law into non-law, or at least into inferior law.

All positive legal stipulations which, when violated, do not lead to nullity of the acts concerned, are now turned into mere desires, or, one could say, political postulates; hence, according to the basic tenets of Kelsen's school, they are a juridical nothing whenever the highest agencies do not correct the flaws. However, when, in another instance, the flaw is corrected, it would be hard to deny that the regulations which are violated have legal standing. After all, what could give a higher agency the right to such correction if the legal stipulations did not qualify as merely political wishes or desires? Here we confront the antinomy according to which the construction of "*Fehlerkalkül*" should take a regulation at one and the same time to be law and non-law, an antinomy from which no *Normlogik* on earth can extricate itself.

Once again we are face to face with the antinomy in the starting point of *Normlogik*. After all, the starting point was that the science of law creates law logically, and as it does so it regards empirical laws, ordinances, acts of organs, and so on, as "material" only. But in the theory of "*Fehlerkalkül*" the relationship has been inverted. The science of law becomes passive, while the factor that determines what is law has become the positive legal material. Such is the fatal antinomy in the norm-logical starting-point which, in a general sense, can be traced back to the incongruency of wanting to relate the logically creative character of the science of law to the postulate of legal positivism.

Is it not likely that this entire theory will also show the basic antinomy between the ideal of science and the ideal of personality which we already disclosed above in the naturalistic schools of humanistic legal theory? Indeed, our analysis of the antinomy in the form-content problem already discovered it to be at work. It will appear to us more clearly still. However much the ideal of personality, as an encroachment by the so deeply reviled natural law, may have been

pushed back in legal science, still, when it comes to the problem of legal force, Adolf Merkl is reluctantly compelled to
acknowledge to Fritz Sander the deeper personalistic bent
of the norm-logical theory of law. He makes this admission
(which cannot be flattering to the ostensibly positivistic legal
theory of the Austrian school) in a few footnotes, almost as if
to hide it, in his curious work *Die Lehre von der Rechtskraft*.
Here Sander's view, which shows kinship with Von Bülow's
theory of process according to which all actions by state
organs are law *qua talis*, is stigmatized as state absolutism,
while, by contrast, Merkl crowns his norm-logical theory
with *the world and life view of liberalism*, according to which
the science of law can freely determine the legal character
of acts by state organs, to the point of taking the liberty to
qualify non-appellate acts of state as non-law, as jural nulli-
ties.[52] It is the theory of the liberal "law"-state, with which
the norm-logical theory of legal force, according to Merkl,
shows such genuine kinship. And this admission is accompa-
nied, furthermore, by the incomprehensible, even somewhat
naive, statement that the author has unreservedly, as legal
theoretician, disentangled himself from all ethical-political
prejudice. Hence it must really be considered a happy coincidence that the norm-logical theory accords so wondrously
well with the liberal, humanist world and life view.

With that, we may now take our leave of this humanistic legal theory. Not, however, without emphatically point-
ing out once more that, even in this idealistic type of the
humanistic conception of law, the fundamental antinomy
of the humanistic law-idea, the everlasting conflict between
the science and personality ideals, has shown itself in ways

that are indeed tragic.

2.3 Relativist-personalist types: the Baden School in neo-Kantian legal theory

Up to this point humanists might, with a semblance of justice, accuse us of reprehensible one-sidedness. For we have been concerned only with those humanistic conceptions of law that bear the rationalistic imprint of the humanistic ideal of science on their brow. Did it never occur to you, they will protest, that for some considerable time already this rationalism has met with serious opposition from within the bosom of humanism? Have you not been informed that irrationalist metaphysics has, for some decades now, again taken up the cudgels against this rationalism, and that a flood of philosophies of life is sweeping aside the rigid rationalist universe of concepts? That the world of meaning has been rediscovered in natural reality itself? And that the ideal of personality is slowly but surely pushing back the ideal of science? See Peter Wust, *Der Auferstehung der Metaphysik* (1920).

We can countenance this remonstration without pangs of conscience. For instead of one-sidedly focusing on the rationalistic schools of humanism in order to demonstrate exclusively in those schools the presence of the fundamental antinomy of the humanistic world and life view, our intention was to show how the inner dialectics must continually goad humanism from the primacy of the science ideal back to the primacy of the personality ideal and how the personalistic schools too are affected by the fundamental antinomy.

It is in particular the Baden School of neo-Kantianism

(Wilhelm Windelband, Heinrich Rickert, Emil Lask, et al.) which, in professed appreciation of Fichte's idealism of freedom, once again favors the personality ideal of humanism over against the hypertrophy of the science ideal in the Marburg School.[1] Between the realm of values and that of mathematical nature they have placed the realm of culture, as the realm of meaning, of the realization of values, "*die Werthaltung an der Wirklichkeit,*" the "adhesion to reality." The gap between natural science and cultural science then appears in the formation of historical concepts which derives its hallmark from its theoretical "*wertbeziehende*" (value-relating) and individualizing tendency, in contrast to the "*wertindifferente*" (value-neutral) generalizing and abstracting kind of concept formation practiced in the natural sciences.

The cultural sciences do not themselves level practical value judgments. "Values" are but the object of "*Bekenntnis*" (acknowledgment), not "*Erkenntnis*" (knowledge). Instead, these sciences investigate "values" throughout culture (such as state, moral freedom, law, religion, and so on), values that realize themselves as history unfolds. The cultural sciences do so purely theoretically, without making scientific judgments about the absolute worth of such values as they realize themselves. It is in the curious relation between values and reality—in the realization of values, in the realm of "*Sinngefüge*" (frameworks of meaning), of "*Bedeutungen*" (meanings)— that the cultural sciences have their own special *Gegenstand* as they form their concepts. It is an intermediate realm, a relationship between Kant's two worlds, between the world of being (*Sein*) and the world of ought (*Sollen*).

Remark: It was in his important rectorial oration, *Geschichte und Naturwissenschaft* (1894) that Wilhelm Windelband developed the program of the Baden philosophy of science, which was later worked out in masterly fashion by his pupil Heinrich Rickert.

In the empirical sciences Windelband distinguished between nomothetic and ideographic disciplines, which was meant to replace the distinction between the natural sciences and the humanities as defended by Wilhelm Dilthey. The nomothetic sciences have as their ultimate goal to search for what is general only, for abstract laws in a natural-scientific sense. The ideographic sciences, by contrast, with the discipline of history as their example, aim at describing that which is particular and "unrepeatable" (*einmalig*), what is typical of values ("*werttypisch*") This distinction is not of a material, physical nature. To a certain degree, for example, the ideographic approach extends into the domain of the natural sciences (consider Darwinism as a biological theory of evolution). On the other hand, the nomothetical approach can also intervene in the science of history and the other humanities. From this it appears that the distinction between nomothetic and ideographic is purely *formal*. It provides the alternate viewpoint from which the material of empirical science can be understood.

Now then, these ideas were deepened in an epistemological sense and further developed by Rickert. Of fundamental significance here is his epistemological work, *Der Gegenstand der Erkenntnis*, 3rd ed. (1915), in which the primacy of the personality ideal is carried through also in the foundations of logic.

According to Rickert, the basic problem of epistemology is *the problem of transcendence*. This is the problem of the "object of knowledge" that is located beyond the transcendental or formal-logical consciousness ("consciousness as such" as a limiting concept, "which alone can never be an object or belong to the contents of consciousness"). This "object of knowledge" cannot be the ontic "*Ding an sich*," for according to transcendental idealism all ontic being is found within consciousness. Through a sharp analysis of the essence of knowledge Rickert arrives, entirely in line with Windelband, at the conclusion that the only transcendent element of knowledge, and thus the only "object of knowledge," is the norm that meets the value of truth.

All knowledge is *judgment*, is an *affirmation* or *negation*, and every affirmation or negation is assuming an alternative position vis-à-vis a value or a non-value. In respect of its "achievement" knowledge itself is therefore to be viewed as an evaluation.

On the basis of his theory of judgment, Rickert proceeds to distinguish three logically independent spheres, namely

1) the sphere of *reality* (to be understood as reality inside the consciousness);

2) the sphere of *values*, which do not have real existence but can only *obtain*;

3) the sphere of "meaning" ("*Singefüge*," "*Bedeutung*")
which the judgment possesses as "achievement" for
grasping the true (immanent, subjective) meaning,
as opposed to the transcendent, objective meaning
that coincides with the transcendent value.[1a] This
domain of immanent, subjective meaning establishes the relation between the sphere of reality and the
sphere of validity of values.

On the basis of this epistemology Rickert elaborated
Windelband's distinction between nomothetic and ideographic sciences in the fourth and fifth edition of his
work, *Kulturwissenschaft und Naturwissenschaft* (1921);
again, in his more encompassing work *Die Grenzen
der naturwissenschaftlichen Begriffsbildung*, 2nd impr.
(1913); and finally, in his major work, *System der Philosophie* (1921).

While maintaining the terms "nomothetic" and
"ideographic" to designate the methodologies, Rickert
replaced these terms by speaking of the "natural" sciences and the "cultural" sciences. The natural sciences
always search for laws or general concepts. The cultural
sciences, of which the science of history is the archetype,
proceeds in an *individualizing* way: in opposition to the
generalizing method of the natural sciences it brings to
the fore the *heterogeneity* of reality in its continuity. What
the individualizing method of the cultural sciences does
have in common with the generalizing method of the
natural sciences is that by applying the transforming
instrument of the concept it changes the *continuity* of

reality into a *discontinuity*. Yet in this *discretum* a cultural science now tries to grasp in its concepts not what is general, but what is particular and heterogeneous.

Now then, while the concepts of natural science constantly strive to be of broader range along with narrower content, historical concepts by contrast strive to be ever closer to individuality. (That Rickert did not understand the essence of the modern logic of relations has been demonstrated by Cassirer in the first chapter of his work of 1923, *Substanzbegriff und Funktionsbegriff*, entitled "Zur Theorie der Begriffsbildung.") In the meantime, Rickert has conceded that the science of history in a relative sense does contain elements of natural science. While in this way the principle of particularization, of *heterology*, is introduced into neo-Kantian epistemology, this individualization, on the other hand, must reach for a unity postulate. This unity in historical concept formation is established through *Wertbeziehung*, i.e., by relating to values, by linking what is *einmalig* (unique) to cultural values. In the cultural sciences we are interested in what is individual only insofar as it relates to specific cultural values. Thus, the method of concept formation here is *teleologically individualizing*; thought here has a theoretical focus on the "relation to values," not a practical focus on evaluating. Thought does not begin to evaluate until it tests the cultural facts against self-existent objective values, which turn into *oughts* by subjectivizing them into norms.

For this reason, the Baden School will have no truck with modern historicism that reifies a temporal *realization* of values to the rank of a value. As Emil Lask had remarked: "Historicism is nothing but an empirical-scientific method that presents itself as a worldview, an inconsistent, uncontrolled, and dogmatic mode of evaluating. In that respect it is no different from naturalism."[2]

[End of Remark]

This school also counts adherents in the field of the science of law (among others, Georg Jellinek, Gustav Radbruch, Emil Lask, Leonhard Cohn, Hermann Kantorowicz, Gamschei Wielikowski, Walter Staffel, Fritz Münch, and Max Weber,[3] and, at an earlier stage, Julius Binder). Accordingly, the science of law becomes a science of culture that must consider law not as a mere "is," nor as an absolute norm, but rather as a relation of reality to the absolute law-idea, as a specific "*Sinngefüge*" (framework of meaning).[4] It should not attempt, as Stammler did, to found the science of law on the *concept* of law, and then, next to it, have legal philosophy provide a wholly independent evaluation of positive law with reference to the absolute law-idea. No, positive law, a cultural phenomenon from the start, relates to the *idea* of law; the concept of law can only be derived from the idea of law. And the value and force of law is not a merely formal idea, as Stammler would have it, but has a material content.[5]

To characterize this species of legal theory, we would like to linger for a moment at Radbruch's conception of law, seeing as it is the most systematic application of the ideas of the Baden School to the science of law and legal philosophy. Later, we shall devote some attention to Binder's comprehensive system of legal philosophy (which has clearly made the transition to objective idealism).

Radbruch gives an account of the essence and task of legal science and legal philosophy in his polished *Grundzüge der Rechtsphilosophie*.[6]

Taking his cue from the Baden philosophy, Radbruch sees law as a cultural object; it lies neither in the realm of natural reality, nor in that of values, nor in that of religion which transcends the contrast of value and non-value.

Law first acquires meaning by its relation to the value of justice, just as the cultural fact of science first gains meaning by its relation to the value of truth, and the cultural fact of positive morality by its relation to the value of personality or virtue. As substrate to the value of justice it is involved in the "is"-sphere, but in terms of its meaning, its "*Bedeutung*," it is the object of normative evaluation. The concept of law, although its content may be attained in an empirical manner, can only be "philosophically founded" through the idea of law, by its relation to the value of law.[7] People's sense of right is only possible by relating positive law to the value of law.

Having arrived at this crucial point, Radbruch candidly lays bare the unresolved antinomy of the humanistic law-idea. Science, after all, cannot itself confirm values: values are only amenable to acceptance, not to scientific demonstration. The value of law as the purpose of positive law is only one of many values: in addition to the community value of justice we find two other groups of values: the personal value of morality, and the operative values of truth and beauty (science and art).

These values must not be left unreconciled next to each other. Their coordination must become subordination. One of the values must be accepted as absolute, writes Radbruch, and only personality can make the choice.

Scientifically speaking, the three possible groupings must be considered each other's equivalent. Each is typified by a specific slogan: freedom, power, or culture. At least the first two are reflected in certain political systems (liberalism and democracy on the one hand and conservatism on the other). *Philosophical relativism*, of which Radbruch, like his mentor Jellinek, shows to be an adherent, can reserve only a twofold task for a scientific consideration of the value of law: one is inquiry into the proper means that are to lead to the realization of the once accepted purpose of law (this is the task of politics); the other is inquiry into the whole range of possible purposes of law (that is the task of legal philosophy). Although legal philosophy cannot decide debates about the purposes of law in a scientific sense, it can prepare the personal choice by indicating the political consequences of an opinion, the world and life view that it presupposes, and, finally, its systematic relation to other political convictions. Only by way of a comprehensive inquiry into all possible points of view can the content of the value of law be fully understood.[8] But how can the concept of law orient itself to the value of law in a universally valid scientific manner if the choice of this value's content is left entirely to personal conviction?

One senses the clash here between the ideal of science and the ideal of personality. The human personality must not be enslaved under the tyranny of continuity inherent in the humanist ideal of science. It must push this ideal of science from the realm of culture, where it is to establish a new concept of science, one that can hem in the universal-mathematical concept of science. But if the personality will not be subject to laws, how can this new concept be established at all, except on quicksand, which will give way at the first attempt to establish a footing? Radbruch did discover this antinomy between personality and science ideal, but now he tries to resolve it in a most curious manner. There is no reason to fear, he writes, that the concept of law, because of its orientation to the idea of law, will be caught up in the relativistic uncertainty of this idea. For, no matter how one wishes to define the idea of law, its substrate and, with that, the concept of law, will always remain fixed.[9]

But this scientific optimism on Radbruch's part is dumbfounding. For we have just been told that the concept of law cannot be a concept of nature, that law does, in its lower part (if we may put it this way) reach into the sphere of *Sein*, as a substrate for the value of law, but that as to its meaning—according to its "*Bedeutung*"—it is not nature but "*Wertbeziehung*" (value-relation). How can we gain any scientific certainty in this way about the concept of law? What use is it to know that law in its natural aspect cannot be influenced by value-relativism? The concept of law as a cultural concept will most certainly be cast adrift from its scientific moorings by this relativism!

Indeed, the antinomy we have seen to be at work in a different, logicistic form in the norm-logical conception of Kelsen, lurks right here in the conception of the concept of law as a concept of relation. The category of law has been relativized; it is not anchored in an absolute modality as the sovereign law-quality of the jural angle of approach. Thus, the relation between the *Sein* of nature and the *Sollen* of the realm of Kantian freedom has taken on the character of an unmistakable antinomy.

Critical neo-Kantianism cannot escape the basic question of Kant's criticism. In all of nature the continuity of the law of causality obtains. How then, is a realization of values in nature itself possible, as object of scientific knowledge? Rickert, who has considered this question most seriously, concludes with an "*ignoramus et ignorabimus*": we don't know, and we'll never know. He puts the question as follows: How is the power of values over reality to be understood? In what way can we comprehend how values are the cause of culture? His answer: In no way whatsoever. Valid *thought* is tantamount to separating things logically from natural reality. We can understand the "valuing act" as a relation between values and culture, which is most significant for understanding the meaning of our lives; but we cannot understand the values that obtain as also being the cause, nor can we comprehend its power over reality. For then the one and the other would be fused in the unity of identity: the concepts of being and of validity would be submerged into each other. Here we find ourselves at the limiting boundary of all scientific understanding, and this insight presumably is the "solution" to the problem.[10]

But this sceptical "resignation" can satisfy no orthodox Kantian, nor any person who wants to think scientifically.

For, to posit a theoretical relation between two realms that is founded on nothing, two realms which, in Kant, are each other's antithesis, means to create an antinomy in a third, intermediate realm. The Baden School cannot indicate a logical limit between natural and cultural science. Neither "*Wertbeziehung*" nor individualization can delimit historical concept formation. After all, natural science too evaluates and individualizes, while the historical sciences, on the other hand, cannot make do without typification and without laws. At best one could, as Paul Oppenheim has recently done, speak in this case of a gradated or a polar distinction.[11] But then the fundamental antinomy between the continuity drive of the science ideal and the ideal of personality continues unabated. If this antinomy lurks even in Radbruch's concept of law, that is, in the entire basis of the science of law, then how many antinomies will not arise from this wellspring the moment one undertakes a serious construction upon this foundation? The supposed firmness of the concept of law is soon submerged in the relativistic uncertainty of the idea of law, and, with that, the science of law itself will be set adrift.

Since Radbruch takes the position that the concept of law cannot depend on the question what content is to be accorded to the idea of law or what position is to be given to the value of law in the system of values,[12] he finds it sufficient for the transcendental determination of the concept of law to orient it to one of the possible ideas of law. The systematization of values, which *ultimately determines the value of law*, must adhere, he writes, to two criteria, namely their nature and their rank. The differentiation of values takes place according to the first of these criteria. Lask's theory of *"Bedeutungs-differenzierung"*[13] (differentiation according to meaning) has demonstrated the probable truth of the thesis that variety *in kind* of values is determined by the variety of substrates to which they point. According to rank, values order themselves into a hierarchy of *original* and *derivative* (directly or indirectly derived), *dominant* and (in various degrees) *serving* values, a graduated succession of goals and means.

The value of law, according to Radbruch, cannot be ranged among the three commonly accepted original values: morality, truth, and beauty. Therefore law must be considered one of the *derivative* values, one of the *serving* values whose task it is—like apostles in the service of the trinity— to expand the rule of these original values to cover the whole world and to furnish reality (seeing as reality is not itself in a position to be a bearer of an absolute value) with a value as a means to realize absolute value. Two kinds of material can be made to serve the realization of those highest values: natural forces and human forces, things and persons, capital and labor. The realization of values in nature is dealt with in philosophy of nature and technology in the widest sense, while the realization of values in humanity is dealt with in four philosophical disciplines, namely:

1. *pedagogy*, whose object is the realization of values in individual lives in successive phases;

2. *psychical dietetics*, whose object is the realization of values in the life of the individual and the coexistence of inclinations;

3. *philosophy of history*, which deals with the realization of values in the life of communities in successive generations;

4. *legal philosophy and politics*, which deal with the realization of values in the life of the community and the coexistence of its members.[14]

In this way, it would seem, Radbruch has found the place of legal philosophy in the classification of philosophical disciplines, as well as the place of the idea of law in the system of values according to one of the possible hierarchies. The idea of law is the specific value of the regulation of the life of the community. That supposedly determines the concept of law as that of *community regulation*.

Very well, let us ascertain whether this definition will suffice to extricate the concept of law from the quicksand of Radbruch's relativism.

In his closer analysis of the concept of law our author rejects Kelsen's conception of law according to which the legal obligation is primary, and subjective right is but a function of legal obligation.[15] By contrast, Radbruch opts for the view of Professor Leon Petrazyck of St. Petersburg,[16] who believed that via psychological analysis he could establish the distinctive feature of law to be its *imperative and attributive* nature—the necessary correlation of right and obligation rather than the purely obligatory nature of ethical norms. Subjective right does exist *through* legal obligation, but not *for the sake of* that obligation. Primacy belongs to subjective right, not to the obligation. Law can serve morality only by giving rights to the individual in order that he be better able to fulfill his obligations. Think of the justification of the right of ownership that was attempted by this school. Legal obligation therefore exists for the sake of moral duty.

Let us pause for a moment to note that this analysis of the concept of law has nothing to do with a scientific analysis, but rests entirely on the scientifically unprovable hypothesis of the primacy of the value of personality in the system of values, as Radbruch himself points out.

Kelsen, who accorded primacy to the ideal of science, could not, on this standpoint, save subjective right.[17] Scientifically speaking, no judge can decide which side is correct. At this point already, the concept of law appears to be bogged down in the quicksand of relativism.

But let's carry on. As he continues his analysis, Radbruch comes to discuss the tenability of Kelsen's distinction between law and morality as a *heteronomous* versus an *autonomous* system of norms.[18] He denies it is tenable, by reason of the fact that a heteronomous obligation, as an obligation imposed by another's will, is self-contradictory. At best, a will can create a *must* but never an *ought*. A legal obligation can exist only as a duty, as a demand, as a norm which the moral personality creates in his conscience. In other words, law can only derive its validity from the validity of morality: the precepts of law are only valid when the moral personality accepts them as norms.

Once again, we discern an encroachment by the relativistic ideal of personality upon the domain of science, an encroachment which creates a fresh, insupportable antinomy: the antinomy between personal liberty in the conscience and the normative restraint of the legal subject by the objective order of law. The jural concept of obligation cannot but fall away. There is no duty other than moral duty. But with its fall the concept of duty takes down with it all the other categories of law (authority, imputation, punishment, guilt, etc.). With one blow law seems relegated again to the realm of causal nature.

For all that, Radbruch's starting point requires that he escape this consequence. The manner in which he seeks to resolve the antinomy created by his personalistic relativism is—remarkable coincidence—essentially the same as that followed in our country by Professor Krabbe of Leiden in his efforts to have positive law spring exclusively from an individual's sense of what is right without thereby surrendering it to an individualism that would make a mockery of all legal order. Given its normative validity, its obligatory nature, law can only be ethics yet can be delimited from ethics by not focusing on the source of validity but on the agency that determines the content of the obligation. In that sense law can indeed be called heteronomous in distinction from morality.

Obligations, after all, must be distinguished in *direct* and *indirect* ethical obligations. The latter are the "cultural obligations" that establish the practical values of truth and beauty as the task of moral conduct, together with numerous duties of social ethics, such as justice and lawfulness, in which, respectively, the so-called "*richtiges Recht*" (right law) and positive law are comprehended as moral goods.

In the case of these *indirect* moral duties, the personality does indeed subject himself to a foreign lawgiver. Personality itself does make justice to be a moral task, but the determination of the content of these goods is left to another agency: to legislation, politics, and legal philosophy. And this determination of content may also come from another's will.

In the case of the *direct*, autochthonous moral duties, the personality that is obligated must also, creatively, produce the content of the duties in his own conscience. By contrast, the *indirect* moral duties allow for the possibility that their content is not determined by the conscience itself. After all, the persons to whom the cultural duties are addressed cannot possibly reproduce humanity's entire cultural achievement artistically and scientifically; they can only pick up the results of the work of others in this realm and make them their own. Such is also true of the content of law and justice.

Meanwhile, this whole argument is hardly compelling. Law here still derives its obligating force, its validity, from acknowledgment by the moral personality alone. The content of legal obligations may be established by the will of a government, but the obligating force of legal precepts nevertheless continues to depend on their congruence (or lack thereof) with the moral norms which the personality acknowledges as such. All law that does not meet this requirement has the nature of empirical force, naked coercion, natural causality. Is the independent nature of law safeguarded in this way?

On the contrary. Law has become the buffer between nature and value. All the antinomies in which the humanistic idea of law has entangled itself seem to find their concentration on one point in the jural sphere.

Not until he discusses the problem of the law's validity does Radbruch take a road that immediately reminds one of Krabbe's psychological justification (*sit venia verbo!*[19]) of the majority principle.[20]

Radbruch distinguishes the jural, the sociological, and the philosophical validity of law. [21] The jural theory of validity remains within positive law itself. It must accept the validity of legal regulations and can only affirm the validity of a legal precept by an appeal to other legal precepts, hence cannot solve the problem of legal validity. The sociological theory of validity, using Jellinek's theory of the "*normative Kraft des Faktischen*" (the normative force of the factual) and Bierling's "*Anerkennungstheorie*" (a theory of acknowledgment), has attempted to base the independent validity of law either in sociological regularity or in acknowledgment by the associated legal persons. The former must fail, since it skips from mere facticity to the normative; the latter leaves the field of sociology the moment it joins Bierling in basing the validity of law on an "*Anerkennungs*sollen" (an "ought" of acknowledgment), not on a factual "acknowledgment" by the legal subjects.

Accordingly, is it then the philosophical theory of validity alone that can bring the problem to a resolution? (Not natural law theory, of course, which establishes the absolute purposes of law, for that would inevitably create an antinomy between natural law and positive law.)

But no, according to Radbruch, curiously enough, it is relativism that must provide the solution to the antinomy that seems to inhere in the problem of legal validity. Presumably, the validity of positive law can be safeguarded precisely by the relativistic belief that the question about the purpose of law can only be answered by the tally of various partisan, factional opinions about it—in other words, by the denial of an absolute natural law. Regulating the life of the community, after all, cannot be left to the legal conceptions of the individual legal associates; that would result in chaos. A supra-individual agency must regulate here. Since reason and science cannot carry out this task, will and power must take on that task. Law does have justice as its more remote goal, but legal security is its more proximate goal. Legal security fully justifies the positive validity of law. The two purposes of law, legal security and justice in all its relativistic multiplicity of meaning, are equally suited for "ethical dress" (a term in Lask)—i.e., fit to be elevated to the level of moral goods.

The result is astounding. Relativism has converted its predicament into a virtue and now appears to rescue the normative character of positive law with the assertion that its own consequences must be rejected. How then, we would ask, is legal security suddenly withdrawn from the basic relativistic thesis? Can relativism really and fully save the obligatory and normative nature of law? Has it committed suicide under the pressures of its antinomies? And does this pseudo-solution to the problem of legal validity not give rise, moreover, to a new antinomy, that between justice and legal security? Is this antinomy to be resolved by abandoning justice as legal value? But does this not mean that the concept of law, which after all needed to be philosophically derived from the idea of law, will suffer the same fate?

Radbruch is aware of the critical position of the ideal of personality. He frankly admits that, where the purpose of law is the concept of law's principle of unity, the concept of law too must break up if two mutually independent purposes are to be assigned to law. Accordingly, he writes, this new antinomy is to be resolved in the sense that both purposes of law, justice and legal security, are subordinated to a communal ideal of law, which, depending on the reigning world and life view, is in turn characterized by the slogans of power, freedom, or culture. The communal purpose of justice and legal security should determine, case by case, which of the two ought to have priority.

In other words, legal security, which, as the purpose of law, was supposed to safeguard the law against relativism, is itself relativized in the end, so as to cause the antinomy to reappear in its original dimensions. For when Radbruch suggests that there is a whole range of political-legal problems that is unaffected by the struggle of world and life views and by politics—such as the protection of property, limitation, legal force, and so forth[22]—he is sorely mistaken. Anarchism and communism, which, in terms of his relativistic viewpoint, cannot be denied their theoretical equivalence to any other world and life view, cannot keep the problems mentioned outside the political struggle. Thus, law after all, in its positivity, is a set of imperatives, a causal phenomenon of power located in Kant's realm of necessity, of natural inevitability. Law can only acquire a normative meaning as ethical duty. The intermediate sphere of culture, in which law is supposed to reside in its cultural meaning, is in fact the buffer of antinomies.

Radbruch's conception of the science of law too is burdened by this fundamental antinomy.[23] In fact, it is exacerbated here and becomes the well-spring of a fresh series of antinomies.

For Radbruch, positive law, the object of the science of law, precisely as positive law, is a set of imperatives. The imperative character of positive law is demonstrated in terms of the problem of freedom. The norm, as valid value, appeals to the free will, the imperative addresses itself as reality to the determinable unfree will; it is psychological coercion, causal effectivity. If we can successfully prove that the world to which positive law belongs is a world of coercion and constraint, of unfreedom, then the imperative nature of positive law has been established beyond a doubt. With an appeal to Henri Bergson, Radbruch now shows that real freedom only exists in "*Erleben*" (experiencing), which is thought-free, so beyond the grasp of any category of thought. Freedom is expressed only in the stream of life. In Kantian fashion, this experiencing of freedom is especially reserved for the area of moral reaction.

Law, however, does not address the individual experience; it does not have as its object man's relation to himself, but social relations. Hence it is directed at constraint. From a positivistic viewpoint this necessarily eliminates the legal character of the concepts of norm-violation, obligation, punishment, retribution, and imputation. These concepts are all ethical in kind. Only as a standard of evaluation does law fall outside determinism's and indeterminism's sphere of predictability. Thus, according to its sociological *Sein*, positive law can be the object only of a causal social-theoretical, sociological approach. Yet at the same time law derives its "*Bedeutung*," its meaning, solely from the "*Wertbeziehung*" to the value of law.

This "*wertbeziehende*" view of law, Radbruch explains, is that of legal theory. Now then, according to its *meaning* the imperative is indistinguishable from a norm. After all, the imperative cannot be defined other than as a will that has an *ought* as its content (*sic*). And since legal theory only abstracts the normative content from the imperative, it ignores the element of will that underlies it. Methodologically then, the science of law cannot be distinguished from a normative science. It proceeds from the realm of *Sein*, from positive laws and legal customs, and yet arrives at results which no longer have the empirical nature of *Sein*.

Just think of the interpretation of a *Rechtssatz*, which must necessarily be philological for the sociologist and the legal historian, but evaluative for the jurist. The legislator's will, as the aim and outcome of judicial interpretation, like the "will" of parties to an agreement, can only be something normative, not a psychical fact. The jural construction reproduces the entire positive legal regulation of a legal institution from its "*Zweckidee*," its *ratio* or purpose, and the legal system is nothing but the reproduction of all law from the

"*Zweckidee des Rechtes*," from its *ratio juris* or purpose. Jural conceptualization is then necessarily teleological. Just as the concept of law is oriented to the idea of law, so also the concept of every separate and distinct legal institution must be derived from its specific purpose.

In all this, legal theory differs from legal philosophy only in this sense that when inquiring into the means by which to achieve the purpose of law legal theory is emphatically bound to the meaning of positive law. The law authentically determines "*richtiges Recht*," i.e., "correct right," or right law.

In this entire conception of the science of law, no matter how much more sympathetic we find it to be than that of Kelsen, we have a proliferation of the fundamental antinomy of the entire system. To begin with, the concept of a psychical will that is supposed to have an *ought* as content is absurd. One cannot *will* an *ought*.

The antinomy of the form-content problem takes on almost grotesque features in Radbruch's concept of culture. The teleological idea which Radbruch imports into the law has no foundation in neo-Kantianism. It destroys the concept of law because it breaches the sphere sovereignty of the jural and in relativist fashion sacrifices the value of law to personal conviction. Where, for Radbruch, the norm can only be ethical in character, and where the moral personality, in the final analysis, will not be bound by the so-called legal purpose of legal security, as we have seen, there Radbruch's theory of interpretation, his view that the jural interpretation is a normative processing of empirical legal material within the limits of the meaning of positive law, is likewise saddled with an inner antinomy.

The conception of law as a concept of culture turns out to be a hybrid monstrosity throughout, a veritable hotbed of antinomies that seeks its support in the original antinomy of the humanistic idea of law: namely, the unresolved conflict between the ideal of science and the ideal of personality.

2.4 Trans-personalist and objective-idealist types

Thus far we have laid bare the peculiar types of antinomies in which naturalistic, critical-logistic, and critical-personalistic humanism could not but ensnare themselves.

However, modern legal philosophy is also witnessing a renaissance, once again, of objective idealism, a trans-personalist legal philosophy which, in conscious alliance with Hegel (albeit with reservations) claims to have overcome the Kantian dualism. It rejects the synthetic form-content problem in the realm of culture and, once again, looks for a final, highest unity, the unity of objective, absolute *Reason* above and beyond every form of dualism or pluralism of law-spheres.

Julius Binder in particular, in his grandly conceived *Philosophie des Rechts*, appears to have made the dialectical switch from subjective to objective idealism within the humanist ideal of law.[1] Initially a student of Windelband and Rickert, Binder sensed the hopelessness of the critical, dualistic position.[2] The basic error of all of neo-Kantianism, according to him, is that it has taken the synthetic form-content problem, which Kant considered meaningful in the realm of nature only, and applies it as well to the realm of culture and normativity. — As if a synthesis of logical category and empirical-sensory material could ever result in the creation of a *Gegenstand* other than that of nature! After all, the understanding can never comprehend anything other than nature, causality, with its categories. What we have here is essentially a new wave of the Enlightenment, however dead it was presumed to be. Modern psychologistic, logicistic and phenomenological positivism wants to understand culture through intellectual operations like those of formal logic, mathematics, or mathematical natural science.[31]

The program of Hegel's objective idealism, namely, to understand the reasonable in the real, must be reopened.[4] The critical question, *How is legal experience possible?* is meaningless in the realm of transcendental reason but not in the realm of objective reason. The very possibility of law, writes Binder, signifies its reasonableness, its being determined by laws of freedom, the ideas.[5] Not by way of critical analysis but by "*Besinnung*" (reflection) or "*Deutung des Gegebenen*" (interpretation of the data) can this critical question be answered. The meaning of the reality of law must be discovered, and before all else one must be aware that its meaning does not consist—as the Baden School still asserted—in a synthesis of category and empirical material, but, instead, belongs totally to the realm of freedom, the realm of validity, of reason, of the spirit. Thus, the world of culture, to which law too belongs, is reality to the extent that it is conceived as subject to certain *a priori* laws or principles of evaluation which do not themselves have a sensory existence, yet which are valid—which point towards reality and in that sense do relate to reality. They do not, as do the categories of the understanding, enter into nature so that they can be abstracted from nature again, but they precede—are prior to—all reality.[6] The ideas then are not, as Hegel asserted, immanent in the world, but neither do they have a merely regulative significance, as Kant argued. They are, writes Binder, the *constitutive principles* of the world of culture. Value relativism must be firmly disavowed. After all, although the ideas of course cannot be known in the same way as empirical facts and processes, yet through reflection we can become conscious of the fact that ideas affect and enter our lives as requirements, as norms, and that by virtue of our consciousness of the obligatory force of these norms, they determine and shape our lives and alone give meaning to our lives. They are the critical conditions without which culture is not possible as reality, as the reality of which we are certain.

Science too is possible only by being subject to such a cultural value. It has its own norm, its own categorical imperative, the "*sein-sollende Wahrheit*" (the ought-to-be truth) which accordingly confronts us categorically, in just as demanding a way as the moral law or the aesthetic norm confronts us.[7] Binder believes that in the unity of all ideas, in the undivided reason that imparts meaning to science as well as morality and aesthetics, we have regained the unity of the world and life view that was lost in Kant's dualism of *Sein* and *Sollen*.

From this brief summary of Binder's philosophical program we can see how humanists once again take the final step available to them in order to solve the basic antinomy in their law-idea. Not only do they accord primacy to the realm of personality, to freedom, but in the final analysis they look for a deeper unity of moral freedom and nature—harmony between the ideal of personality and the ideal of science—in the unity of objective reason.

Just as we were able in the case of the naturalistic, logicistic, and critical-personalistic types of humanistic legal theory, so can we now anticipate in advance the type of antinomies in which Binder's view of law must inevitably become trapped, given the nature of his objective idealism? We think we can, provided we can identify *the type of humanistic law-idea* that underlies this objective idealism.

To do so, however, will not be as easy in the case of Binder as it was with the systems we discussed earlier. His objective idealism, it must be remembered, shows several essential points of difference with that of Hegel and has not been thought through to its ultimate consequences. Rather, it seems that this idealistic system has an admixture of transcendental-critical elements deriving from the Kantian universe of thought.

Binder is fully consonant with Hegel in this respect that he too wants to understand the realm of causal necessity, the realm of nature, as a free act of the spirit, in order thus to escape the antinomy between causality and freedom.[8] He too sees the entire cosmos as subject to the sovereign sway of ideas that find their final unity in objective *Reason*. But Binder denies that the ideas realize themselves in nature and history. He counters Hegel's conception of the immanence of ideas in reality (see, e.g. *Philosophie des Rechts*, p. 866). Binder's ideas are merely "valid." Undoubtedly this is a Kantian legacy in Binder's objective idealism, and along with it comes a second, even more important point of difference with Hegel: Binder accepts a plurality of ideas which he places in a relationship of coordination, side by side. Thus, theoretical truth (the idea of science), the good (the idea of ethics), the beautiful (the idea of aesthetics), and the religious idea (the idea of religion) are all coordinated on the same level. All these ideas, in addition to more ideas that we may be able to discover by the growth of our knowledge, are equally categorical values; they are transcendental as "the absolute, unconditional conditions of reality." They are distinct, final functions of the "transcendental I." Precisely for that reason they cannot be subordinated to each other, as Hegel had done when he made all other values subordinate to the value of truth and so wound up, inevitably, in pan-logicism. What unites values into a unity is exclusively the *Vernunft* or the *Geist* from which they have sprung forth, from *Bewusztsein*.[9]

This critical-Kantian bent in Binder's objective idealism is the source of some most peculiar complications in the humanistic law-idea that underlies Binder's system, and it exacerbates that system's antinomous character. For this time four ideas, and possibly more ideas, and consequently more distinct spheres of law, are placed side by side without any real connection. Binder's thesis that they are all emanations from the same *Geist*, the same *Vernunft*, is incompatible (at least in an objective idealist system) with the idea of their coordination. When Kant isolated *Sein* and *Sollen* from each other, it was because he retained a "*Ding an sich*" and because he wanted to indicate limits for the ideal of science in the interest of the ideal of personality. But idealism arose pre-

115

cisely from the urge to push Kant's humanistic attitude to its full consequences through removing the boundaries between understanding and reason by allowing reason to rule as the creative sovereign also over the realm of the understanding.

As a result, Binder's humanistic law-idea displays a curiously ambivalent attitude. It is based on objective freedom idealism in the trans-personalistic conception of the sovereignty of personality, of the consciousness of freedom. Primacy is given to the ideal of personality, to the *praktischen Vernunft*, and yet science and ethics are not reconciled in the dialectical identity of their ideas. The pluralism of values must end up in a stark antinomy of values, since each value stands on its own and each is accorded absolute categorical control, while the cosmos itself in which these values obtain, in which they determine reality, points instead to an undeniable organic unity.

Everything jars and jolts in this objective idealistic system. Science, especially philosophy, is universally significant. It can cover the areas of ethical and religious ideas, in which case, says Binder, those ideas must bow to the sovereignty of the idea of truth.[10] In terms of his starting point, that is an obvious antinomy. The ideas may also come into conflict with one another. An immoral work of art may very well meet the requirements of the aesthetic idea and yet be flagrantly at odds with the ethical value.[11] Nowhere has an organic harmony, a real reconciliation, been achieved in the realm of ideas. Meanwhile—and that is of special interest to us in connection with the apriori construction of the antinomies in Binder's humanistic legal theory—the postulate of continuity in the trans-personalist sense is energetically put to work in the domain of the separate values. Nature and freedom, coercion and morality, are to be conceived as a continuous coherence of freedom. The freedom of the sovereign personality, objectively understood, must not be imperiled in any way. Legal coercion and morality must therefore be dialectically reconciled. The idea must determine legal reality, otherwise law is not a creation of the free spirit. On the other hand, the idea of law, as a derivative, serving value, must play second fiddle to the ethical idea, or else it will clash with the sovereignty of moral personality. The state with its coercive organization must be taken up in the dialectical reconciliation of coercion and freedom. All this is not just arbitrary theory on Binder's part but follows of necessity from his idea of law which is anchored in the objective idealism of freedom. As a result, sovereign limits of law are violated throughout.

Nor can modern idealism perpetrate such violation with impunity. If our prognosis is correct, Binder's legal philosophy will first of all suffer the effects of the self-inflicted antinomy between the concept of law and the idea of law, madw worse by the effects of the antinomy between positive law and moral freedom. His somewhat Hegelian synthesis between individual-personal freedom and the idea of the state will inevitably founder on the basic antinomy between law and morality which arises when the sovereign limits of these two are transgressed. Here too the legal obligation and, along with it, the inherently normative character of law, will dissolve. In the end, the science of law, too, will become ensnared by the antinomy of values, between truth and moral idea.

We shall now examine how all these antinomies are indeed demonstrably present in Binder's legal theory, and then briefly analyze them.

Given his philosophical starting point, Binder is unable to distinguish legal norms from other norms except by means of the idea of law. Since the constellation of empirical norms and legal institutions exists only for the sake of the idea of law, and since the legal norms owe their "*Dasein*" (existence) and their "*Sosein*" (existing thus) to this idea, the idea of law is the condition for the existence of positive law as well as for its "*Begriffs-merkmal*" (conceptional characteristic), and also, at the same time, its evaluation standard. Thus, the idea of law has both constitutive and regulative significance for positive law. This idea of law may be characterized provisionally as the "*Idee einer Zwangsgemeinschaft unter Menschen*" (the idea of a community of coercion among men).[12]

But even this provisional characterization of the idea of law contains a dreadful antinomy for objective realism. The antinomy between coercion and freedom has here been imported into the primal realm or source of idealistic freedom, into the sphere of ideas itself. We know how Kant too struggled with the selfsame antinomy and how he sought to resolve it with a mathematical, but fallacious argument. Law was said to be "the sum of conditions by which the arbitrariness of the one can co-exist with the arbitrariness of others under a general law of freedom." Well then, a general condition is coercion and retribution. He who violates the law must, as a *homo noumenon*, as co-legislator in the realm of freedom, will his own punishment. By the negation of the negation of law the legal order is maintained in its original sanctity.

Binder cannot adopt this argument unaltered if only by reason of the fact that Kant conceives law individualistically. Binder follows a different road. According to his idea, law is coercion for the individual towards community. Without coercion, community and culture are not possible. Coercion therefore must itself be justified by freedom. At issue here is, essentially, the notorious problem about the relation between law and morality, a problem which Binder has drawn into the sphere of ideas itself.

Rudolf Stammler scrapped the element of coercion in his conception of the idea of law as a "community of freely willing people." Binder intentionally introduces this element into the idea of law itself because for him, unlike for Stammler, the idea of law also contains the constitutive function of the concept of law, so that positive law could not have this compelling character if this element were not part of the very idea of law itself. But how, we may ask, does such an idea of law fit in with the nature of freedom that is supposed to be proper to and inherent in all ideas?

Since Binder, together with all humanism, finds the concept of organic *sphere sovereignty* unpalatable, he can only seek a solution in the relativization of the idea of law. The dualism of law and morality, unbearable to reason's sense of unity, must be resolved, else it would turn freedom itself into an impossible concept. For I know myself to be free only insofar as I am conscious of being subject to the moral law. The realm of freedom must therefore coincide with the realm of morality, and "the transcendental idea of law can only be a case of applying the categorical imperative that controls this realm."[13]

"It is unthinkable that two such laws which are rooted in the same reason should contradict each other, and since they do not coincide in terms of content, there must be some relationship of subordination between them, such that the idea of law subjects itself to the law of morality."[14] In this way the idea of law is degraded to become a serving value, but it remains an idea nevertheless and retains its character of coercion. Coercion is the necessary condition for freedom, hence is perfectly justified in a moral sense, according to Binder.

This entire argument boils down to the thesis that legal coercion is a special application of the idea of moral freedom. Is the antinomy resolved in this way? Hardly. *Humanistic reason starts out by positing its postulate of unity, of continuity; to realize this postulate it goes on to relativize the sovereign law-spheres; and it ends in antinomy.* That is the tragic course of all humanistic thought, whether primacy be granted to the ideal of science or to the ideal of personality. We have ascertained it to be so in both naturalism and neo-Kantianism. Now we must conclude the same to be true of Binder, even though he only applied the postulate of continuity within the limits of each of the absolute values. The concept of "coercion towards the freedom of the moral community" will be encumbered with an inner antinomy, so long as legal sanction and moral freedom are subsumed under the same common denominator of reason. Coercion can never be understood as a special case of the application of humanistic "autonomous" personality. No one, in any reasonable sense, can allow himself to be *forced to be free.*

This idea of law, torn apart by inner antinomy, will, according to Binder, enable us to grasp the concept of all empirical, positive law. Positive law is a teleological relation of means and end, where the means is provided by coercion and the end by the community. Law is not a "*Sollensgemeinschaft*" (a community of moral obligations) but a "*Zwangsgemeinschaft*" (a community of coercion).[15]

The concept of law, too, has become a relation. Not a relation, however, between empirical reality and ethical *Sollen*, as with Radbruch, but a teleological relation of coercion and community in which the terms supposedly determine each other reciprocally. Yet we have seen how the terms here related by the end-means relation do not fall within the same angle of approach at all. Once again, this relation lacks the anchorage of a sovereign, irreducible, modality, and therefore the concept of law as sovereign delimitation of the jural sphere has indeed come to nothing. The element of coercion, as Binder himself admits,[16] was first discovered in empirical reality, since behind all law we find power. To understand this coercion as rational it had to be imported into the idea of law itself, in order subsequently to be projected again into reality from that idea of law as a "*Vernunftgebot*" (a precept of reason). But in this whole train of thought the relation between the idea of law and the concept of law is itself encumbered with an inner antinomy. The idea of law as a function of objective *Reason* creates the law and at once serves as the law's standard of evaluation. A double relation like that between idea of law and positive law, however, is logically absurd. In Hegel's dialectics the ideas realize themselves in reality and posit their own antitheses in it, to resolve them again in syntheses. But Binder has expressly rejected the immanence of Hegel's ideas. The idea itself never becomes empirical but remains in the ideal sphere of freedom. How then can empirical positive law, which is, after all, pure meaning (*"Bedeutung"*), arise from that idea while at the same time the duality between the idea of law and positive law is also retained, as is evident from the second function of the idea of law as a standard by which to evaluate positive law?

Binder's idealism cannot resolve this antinomy; in fact, it cannot even provide so much as a dialectical pseudo-solution, since it has eliminated from Hegel's philosophy its most essential element, the immanence of ideas in reality.

In a tragic monotony, the one antinomy drags the next one after it. In his consideration of the relation of coercion and freedom Binder writes that the reality of law does not consist in a positive legal obligation, but in the "power of the arm of the state," which takes hold of the debtor and executes its will against the "recalcitrant" with inflexible coercion.[17]

Legal duties and obligations, by contrast, do not exist. The duties that the individual has towards the legal order are not rooted in positive law, but in moral consciousness, in moral freedom. "Duties toward the law exist precisely on these grounds; if they were not anchored in the conscience, in the personal *Reason* of the individual, there would be no grounds for duties at all."[18]

The concept of obligation then, is deleted from the law as such. Gone is law's normative character, along with normative categories like imputation, guilt, fault, and so much more. Only as moral categories can they be reintroduced into the law.

It is readily apparent as well that in Binder the law *as such* has remained stuck in the reality of nature. His entire theory of power, which clearly shows him to be a professed adherent of Erich Kaufmann and Hegel's conservative conception of the state, is based on the empirical sensory instruments of power that are the state's, on physical force that coerces the recalcitrant. That this reality of nature is then again ensconced in the realm of ideas by means of the ethical ideal of community, only serves to make the antinomy the more insufferable. Binder writes: "*It may sound paradoxical,* but the legal order, even in its idea, does not presuppose the ideal, but the real human being, and it reckons with him, not as the *homo noumenon* in Kant's sense, but as the empirical human being, with all his weaknesses, his good and his evil will." This paradox, however, is not a seeming paradox, but an insoluble antinomy from which no idealism on earth can extricate itself.

This casts light on the new antinomy which Binder's system displays when he tries to achieve a synthesis between the individual personality and the personality of the state. An individual does not have personality in his empirical "*für sich sein*" (being for himself), but only to the extent that it participates in objective *Reason*. And the latter not only appears in the individual members of mankind, but in all forms of community, thus also in the community of law and state as well. Indeed, only in community does the individual attain to personality.[19] The antinomy of this conception consists in the fact that an individual personality is understood as a moral personality, while, by contrast, the community of the state—in emphatic opposition to Hegel's view—is conceived as a community of law and coercion, not as the highest realization of morality.[20] And now the two heterogenous concepts are again subsumed under one denominator, because humanistic reason simply will not be held back by sovereign limits of law. In consequence, moral personality will inevitably come into conflict with the state's power of coercion. Trans-personalism next attempts to resolve this antinomy by making the individual moral personality dependent upon the idea of jural community. The individual personality is an organic part of the personality of the state. The legal order does not, as the will of the state, confront the individual as a foreign will; rather it is the living will of the people of which the individual is organically a part.[21] In this manner humanistic trans-personalism wants to be the fulfillment of personalism, as indeed it is, to a certain extent.[22]

But this entire so-called trans-personalist conception of the state depends on the possibility of subsuming legal coercion and moral freedom under one denominator.

Where, as has become clear, such is possible only at the expense of an intolerable antinomy, Binder's trans-personalist conception of the state too will be burdened by the selfsame antinomy. Consider:

To this extent, therefore, the power of the jural community over its members has no limits; it is power, pure and simple; and it is entitled to exact any sacrifice from its members. Its limitation is only given with its own Idea: it must not treat the individuals as *mere means,* since such treatment of the legal associates would ruin the community itself and upset the very legal order.[23]

In this statement by Binder the humanistic ideal of personality, after having been transposed into trans-personalism in order to create a higher identity of state coercion with the idea of the free personality, attempts to raise a barrier against the consequence of state absolutism, which is but the result of blurring the boundaries between the jural sphere and the ethical law-spheres.

However—regardless of our own preference for the organic idea—in the idealistic conception of trans-personalism any organic approach has been thoroughly poisoned. There is no remedy in advancing personality itself as a buffer against Hegelian state absolutism, against the absolutistic idea of the cultural state in which the idea of ethical freedom must seek its crowning glory as absolute spirit. Humanism's trans-personal theory of the will removes the last remaining boundaries between individual and community. The will of the community dissolves the will of the individual.[24] That is the consequence of objective idealism, and revealed in it is the antinomy of its starting point which seeks to bring nature and freedom to the higher unity of objective *Reason.*

Given the trans-personal idea of the power-state—which has absorbed the freedom of moral persons in the personality of the state—it is evident that there can be no question of international law, which, after all, does not dispose of the instruments of power. And so Binder's theory of state sovereignty becomes ensnared in the familiar antinomy that the one state cannot recognize the next as equal before the law, since a plurality of equally sovereign states necessarily presupposes a legal order above the states which must regulate their legal relations. But that introduces at once a new antinomy in the unity postulate of reason. In objective idealism reason is not able to comprehend the plurality of states itself as a unity in its idea of an ethical community. It does not help at all to state, as Binder does, that he wants international regulations to be seen as an ethics of states, valid as international morality.[25] For, according to his own conception, coercion is a necessary means, a *sine qua non*, for the realization of the idea of community.

In view of all this, it need not surprise us to witness a re-entry of the "double morality,"[26] which essentially is but a capitulation to a self-created antinomy between law and morality.

The idea of power, seemingly imported into the idea of law merely as a means towards the goal of community, unmistakably shows idealism's basic antinomy between state law and international law. Objective idealism in its entirety seeks to reconcile nature and freedom, and in doing so it violates the sovereign limits between nature, law, and morality, as is apparent from the antinomy between constitutional and international law—all for the sake of the continuity of reason. The ideal of continuity in its Kantian restriction has merely been ascribed to reason instead of to the understanding.

Finally, as far as the predicted antinomy in Binder's conception of the science of law is concerned, we can note that Binder basically hews to the Baden School on this matter, except for this difference that he does not see culture (to which law too belongs) as a synthesis of nature and value but as a completely independent part of reality dominated by practical ideas and separate from nature. The science of law, as a practical science, is then a historical interpretative science whose method must follow the teleological idea of law. But here arises the antinomy with the theoretical value of truth, before which the idea of law too must bend, according to Binder—the very thing it cannot do by virtue of his value pluralism. Binder's distinction between practical and theoretical legal science, which, he says, cannot relate to each other as an antinomy,[27] conflicts with his own tenet according to which all science is only and solely governed by the theoretical idea of truth. This antinomy too is insoluble in Binder's objective idealism.

CHAPTER 3

THE ANTITHESIS BETWEEN THE HUMANIST AND THE CALVINIST LAW-IDEA

REFLECTION ON THE fundamentals of the humanistic world and life view has led us to identify the general structure of a law-idea. Despite the seemingly most diverse, indeed even antithetical, elaborations given to this law-idea, it nevertheless continued to exhibit two constant elements: the ideal of personality, and the ideal of science, even as these two elements alternate in being accorded primacy.

> **Remark**: Ever since the Renaissance, the notion of a law-idea as the foundation of every world and life view has, outside Christian circles, been pushed to the background, even though unconsciously it remains the metaphysical starting point. It is noteworthy that more recently humanists too are in search of a law-idea as the foundation of all speculation about questions of life and the world. As an example I refer to the recent work of the well-known legal philosopher, teacher of penal and process law, Wilhelm Sauer, *Grundlagen der Wissenschaft und der Wissenschaften* (1926). This work, written with excessive

self-estimation, presents as an original idea what is essentially nothing but a renewal of Leibniz' metaphysics, in which the primacy of the science ideal is exchanged for the primacy of the personality ideal.

Sauer's system is built upon two basic conceptions: the *Grundgesetz* (basic law), and the *Wert-monaden* (value monads). Sauer's formulation of the law-idea is instructive: "The basic law of culture affirms the concurrence of the totality of value monads. It is the law-conformative frame of supreme harmony and order. This all-encompassing order must now branch out below into multiple individual orderings, each of which in turn naturally embodies a self-contained whole (albeit it merely smaller)" (p. 70). With this the humanistic idea of culture is introduced in the law-idea while the science ideal is made subservient to the personality ideal. *"All disciplines come round to the cultural point of view; no less the natural sciences,* including mathematics and logic (p. 121). *"The basic law of value is the law of freedom"* (p. 92n). Sauer now permeates the *nature* monad of Leibniz (which revealed the primacy of the science ideal) with the personality ideal and turns it into a *value* monad.

This remarkable work closes with the creed of a pantheistic, humanistic philosophy of culture, and I quote: "But thus speaks the World Spirit: Blessed are the dead which die in *Kultur*. They shall rest from their labors, for their works follow them" (p. 429) (*sic*).

See also by the same author, *Grundlagen der Gesellschaft* (1924), which is built on the same basic idea as his *Philosophie der Zukunft* (1923).

[End of Remark]

Whoever has fathomed this rock-bottom structure of the humanistic law-idea intuits at once that any world and life view built on this foundation must come into irreconcilable conflict with the most fundamental convictions of Christianity. After all, regardless of the temporal shapes in which the Christian world and life view might appear—i.e., regardless of the differences between the main types of Catholicism, Lutheranism, Calvinism and the sects, regardless of the fact that here too pluriformity predominates—, nevertheless those who are Christians in more than name have but one foundation in common, a foundation that differs altogether from the humanistic one.

The common confession that all Christians share contains recognition of God's sovereignty and divine providence, of sin and redemption through Jesus Christ, and of living our temporal existence in the light of eternity. Christianity, in short, believes in the subjection of all creatures, in thought and will, not to the idea of sovereign personality or the notion of sovereign reason, but to the triune God, the Lord of heaven and earth. In the past, whenever humanism and Christianity formed a partnership and Christianity allowed itself to be influenced by humanism, the Christian world and life view became embroiled in antinomies that were even more insufferable than those entailed in the foundation of humanism itself. Worse, the Christian elements were overgrown and eclipsed by the humanistic ones, with the result that Christian thought showed all the symptoms of asphyxiation—as the Age of Enlightenment can teach us as a permanent warning for the future.

Similar to the basic structure of the humanistic law-idea, the Christian law-idea likewise has two constant elements which, despite differences in their elaboration, may be discovered in all its various types: [1] the confession of God's sovereignty as Creator constituting the deepest origin and ground of the validity of all laws that regulate creation; and [2] the confession of God's providence as the organic coherence which integrates all laws to constitute a deeper unity. When various Christian sects lack a real law-idea, it does not mean that they have abandoned these two basic elements, but only that from indifference to *a world lost in sin*, and through a one-sided concentration of their energies on *the life to come*, they neglected to employ these elements for the construction of a comprehensive world and life view.

It was Augustine, in his conception of the *lex aeterna* (the eternal law), who first gave a comprehensive specification of the Christian law-idea. The two basic elements of all Christian thought were suffused with Neoplatonic ideas, but the sovereignty of the will of God pervaded his law-idea above everything else.[1]

Thomas Aquinas, using Augustinian, Aristotelian, and Arabic elements, elaborated the concept of *lex aeterna* into a law-idea which to the present day provides Roman Catholicism with a world and life view of imposing consistency and which integrates into a strict organic unity its ecclesiology, systematic theology, conception of science and scholarship, and its legal and political theory.

The Thomist law-idea, the *lex aeterna*, has shaped the Christian element of divine sovereignty in this sense that divine reason is the author of the providential plan for the cosmos and that in the *lex naturalis* human nature participates in this divine reason, with the result that in the entire natural realm man, by his own rational capacity, can know what the *lex aeterna* has ordained. The second element, that of divine providence, was infused by Thomism with the Aristotelian idea of entelechy: the idea of the twofold goal-orientation of all creatures, in accordance with their own specific nature, towards their own perfection and towards the final purpose of creation. It was a conception that was readily joined by the Augustinian, Neoplatonic idea of the graduated ordering of the universe into higher and lower spheres.

This universal law-idea, if not materially, at least formally, reconciled nature and grace in the teleological idea of entelechy. Nature became the *preambulum gratiae*, the gateway to grace. *Gratia naturam non tollit, sed perficit:* Grace does not abolish nature, but perfects it.

State and law too were now incorporated into this organic conception. Founded in human nature, regulated by the *lex naturalis*, they were subordinated to the church (the institution of grace) as temporal instruments serviceable to man's eternal purpose.

Gradually eroded by schools of nominalism in the Middle Ages, the Thomist law-idea could not but appear as unsatisfactory to the Reformers, since it not only constituted the basis of the Catholic hierarchy and Rome's theology, but it had also imported Aristotelian philosophy into the Christian world and life view.

Luther's passionate soul led him to break clean away from the "*Vermittlungsgedachte*" (idea of mediation) by which Rome had reconciled nature and grace philosophically. Nature, lost in sin, was inclined to all evil and incapable of any good. Luther taught that redemption could enter the world from divine grace alone, without the cooperation of nature. The sovereignty of God's will over all of creation was once again wrested free from the rationalistic overgrowth of Aristotelian philosophy. And as long as this sinful world lasts, the Christian too must bow to the natural ordinances and laws of God. In his natural vocation, in worldly callings, the Christian is to show what grace can do.

Meanwhile, despite his emphasis on the sovereignty of the divine will, it cannot be denied that for the practice of life Luther put too much emphasis on personal deliverance out of this world. He sought God's honor in the world too exclusively in the personal life of love, and, owing to the unbridgeable cleft (to his mind) between nature and grace, he tended to lose sight of the organic coherence of all God's ordinances. The idea of predestination, which Luther emphatically adhered to, was not for him, as it was for Calvin, a holy passion and a restless stimulus to demand acknowledgment of God's sovereignty in all areas of life—to reclaim nature itself for Christ. Lutheranism continued to reflect a cleft in its world and life view, a breach between nature on the one hand and the personal life of grace on the other. In the natural order God's sovereignty was regarded too much in a one-sided way as power, while in personal life it was seen too one-sidedly as love. Luther's dualistic morality of public office and personal ethics (which he was to abandon later), the one-sided accentuation of the element of power in his view of law and state, the more or less quietist view of history according to which the Christian must acquiesce in all that has historically come to be, the depreciation of the idea of law in favor of the idea of personality—they are ever so many testimonies to the weak, unsatisfactory structure which the Christian law-idea displays in its Lutheran conception.

Remark: These traits returned in Stahl's legal philosophy. The law-idea in which Stahl's view of law is anchored is the idea of a "moral world order," a realm of personality in which the person of God is sovereign. The state is also a moral realm, just as in the highest sense of the word God's kingdom is a moral realm. Now then, just as in the kingdom of God the personal dominion of God rules, so also in the state a personal dominion is established over people. Thus, it is most natural that governmental authority centers on a natural personality (the monarch). In a *monarchy* the state becomes personal (the *monarchical principle!*). But here too, governance serves intellectual-moral ends, wherefore here too, people ought to obey in freedom, in that the order over them at once constitutes their own true essence and will.

All this reveals the one-sided personalistic trait of the Lutheran world and life view, *a personalism which, for all that, must in no way be confused with the humanistic personality ideal.*

Lutheranism's historical quietism is evident in Stahl's ripened conception of *Gottes Fügung in der Geschichte"* (God's guidance in history), as well as in his theory of legitimacy and in his almost mystical veneration of that which has come to be in a historical-organic sense.

It cannot be denied that under the influence of Stahl the Lutheran spirit also permeated anti-revolutionary politics [in our country], even though from the very beginning the modern Calvinist school of political theory, pioneered by Groen van Prinsterer, pointed to the difference between the Lutheran and the Calvinist theory of authority; wrote Groen: "Stahl was a Lutheran; I remained a Calvinist." Cf. Groen's beautiful in memoriam, *Ter nagedachtenis van Stahl* (1862). See also D. P. D. Fabius, *Het Wezen van het Calvinisme* (1919).

In addition, I refer to my *Calvinisme en natuurrecht* (1925), pp. 18ff. Any critical purification of the anti-revolutionary political theory on a Calvinist foundation would have to commence with an analysis of the type of Christian law-idea that lies at the foundation of the different schools of this theory. From that point of view, the publication in 1911 of the well-known doctoral thesis by A. C. Leendertz, *De grond van het Overheidsgezag in de antirevolutionaire staatsleer* was a disappointment. When a scholar arms himself with the Kantian distinction between *Sein* and *Sollen* and then directs his entire intellect to those points in anti-revolutionary political theory where this Kantian criterion is violated, he can have an easy time of it. One can know in advance, even without a detailed investigation of the anti-revolutionary theories, that across the board these theories *cannot but* contradict the critical humanistic "isolation" of *Sein* ("being") in opposition to *Sollen* ("ought to be"). Those who proceed in their criticism in this manner are not exercising *immanent criticism* but an *unfruitful transcendent criticism* on the basis of the humanistic standpoint. Given that Kant's separation of *Sein* vis-à-vis *Sollen* essentially indicates nothing but a fruitless attempt to escape from the basic antinomy in the general structure of the humanistic law-idea, those within the Christian camp should be a little more hesitant in uncritically accepting the Kantian dilemma. History has shown that a synthesis between Christianity and Humanism is never made with impunity.

[End of Remark]

Moreover, when Melanchthon, who was keenly aware of the flaws in the Lutheran conception of natural life, sought to rectify matters with the aid of Stoic and Aristotelian philosophy—when he wished to provide an all-encompassing significance once again to the Christian law-idea and employed the (misunderstood) Aristotelian concept of entelechy, nominalistically denatured[2]—then, in so doing, the spiritual gains of the Reformation were partly lost, while the gates of Christianity were opened for the invasion of humanistic ideas.[3]

137

Very well, has Calvinism perhaps developed that universal law-idea which gives our world and life view the constancy and certainty it requires—the idea which in our thought and action draws that clearcut, purposeful line that we need in order to stand firm in the struggle against the world, also in the area of science and scholarship?

Do not underestimate the importance of this question, for upon the answer depend the legitimacy and the possibility of Calvinist science and Calvinist scholarship. Calvinist legal and political theory, too, which Kuyper's genius considered indispensable parts of the cultural task of Calvinism in modern times,[4] will stand or fall with the establishment of a law-idea that will integrate thought and faith, religion and science, view of nature, society, law and morality in one organic unitary structure and cause them to coexist in harmony!

Now then, and it is from the deepest conviction of my soul that this confession springs: Yes, Calvinism possessed such a unity from the beginning. I do not have to uncover it for you, since this law-idea lives in your own soul. In the past it provided Calvinism with unity and clarity in its world and life view; it was intuitively expressed in so many tenets, also in our constitutional and political views; it is the awe-inspiring, vital conception that penetrates all our thought and action, without which Calvinism would have been unthinkable in the past and is bound to be powerless in the future.

Allow me, in the time that remains, to try and indicate, in bold outline, the significance of this our law-idea for the science of law and legal philosophy. The law-idea that underlies the Calvinist world and life view is rooted in the two foundations of all Christian reflection: the confession of the divine Creator's sovereignty, and the confession of the divine providential cosmic plan.

In the elaboration of these basic tenets the following features figure most prominently:

1. The weighty conception of divine sovereignty as the unfettered sovereignty of God's holy will over all areas throughout the whole of creation;

2. The conception of the law in every area as the *boundary* for all human thinking and willing;

3. The absolute subjection of all that is creaturely to the ordinances established by God;

4. The exalted sovereignty of God above these laws;

5. The rejection of every form of theodicy that sets itself up as judge of God's governance of the world.

Closely associated with this idea of the limiting character of the law is the universal doctrine of *sphere sovereignty*, assigning the mutual relationships between the law-spheres that are joined in an organic coherence in the law-idea.

It is this teaching of sphere sovereignty in particular that evokes humanism's continuing opposition to it, owing to the structure of its own law-idea. For, an equal sovereignty of each law-sphere within its own distinct orbit militates most definitely against both the postulate of the sovereignty of reason and the postulate of the sovereignty of personality. History shows that the tendency to construct continuity repeatedly blurred the boundaries of the law-spheres' delimited spheres or proper orbits, which resulted in those insoluble antinomies in the science of law and political theory of which we have just analyzed a few types.

To confess sphere sovereignty is to push human thinking and willing back to indissoluble, absolute boundaries, and to destroy the unrestricted sovereignty of reason and personality alike.

To the human mind, each law-sphere is marked off from the others by an absolute and qualitative boundary. To understand such a law-sphere scientifically, thought must begin by subjecting itself and bowing to the sovereign quality of law in which God's sovereignty as Creator expresses itself directly, without "*Vermittlung*"—without the mediation of other law-spheres.

The distinct quality of each law-sphere impresses itself on our consciousness only by way of intuitive reflexion. For theoretical consciousness they establish fields of vision in which their sovereignty is guaranteed by the quality of law as *a modality of the law-idea*. It is through these modalities that we become aware of the sovereign law-spheres; and the sovereignty of the sphere of scholarship consists in this, that in accepting the fields of vision, it will penetrate them by logical categories of relation and system, and thus will seek to understand them as the strict unity of a logos coherence— an endless task beyond question, in which reflexive thought makes headway only with difficulty. The field of vision en-

closed within the logical categories of identity and diversity, becomes the focus of our thinking, and the Gegenstand
becomes an object, a system of relations determined by the
modality in question.

But when we have understood sphere sovereignty in this
sense, epistemologically, we have still gained only provisional
clarity concerning this profound idea. For it has not yet become clear how the sovereignty of a plurality of law-spheres
can be reconciled with the organic idea of unity which we
have acknowledged as basic to every Christian law-idea. This
difficulty is resolved, however, when we see sphere sovereignty as *flowing from Calvinism's organic law-idea*.

The organic law-idea itself must come to expression in
every sovereign sphere, must penetrate it and provide it with
reality, otherwise the entire doctrine will be but an impossible abstraction, an inner antinomy, not just for our thinking
but for our faith as well.

The law-idea permeates the sovereignty of every sphere
in such a way that it maintains the connection of every law-
sphere with the other law-spheres, something that is incomprehensible to reason in the logical sense. It does so in the
cosmological sense by recognizing that for each of the more
complex law-spheres the earlier spheres serve as its *substrata*;
and it does so in the *epistemological* sense by maintaining
the *analogies* of the earlier law-spheres in the next sovereign
modality of such a law-sphere, analogies which, albeit *in
subjection to the sovereign modality*, build on the substrata in
question.[1]

---

1. [The term "analogies" was later replaced by "retrocipations," in contrast to the "anticipations" discussed next].

Conversely, the Calvinist law-idea teaches us that even the least complicated law-spheres harbor *anticipations* within their field that point ahead to the later, more complicated law-spheres. They are the correlates of the analogies.

This explains, for example, how mathematics can anticipate natural science, and also how natural science, even in its most basic modality (*viz.* energy) maintains mathematical analogies that justify infinitesimal calculus. This helps us to grasp how sociology, for example, can anticipate the normative jural law-sphere, while, conversely, the science of law encounters, within the jural sphere itself, sociological analogies that are based on the sociological substrates of the jural.

In this way the analogies and anticipations in each law-sphere maintain the *cosmic continuity* of the divine cosmic plan, while, equally, sphere sovereignty creates a *logical discontinuity* that can only be bridged at the expense of antinomies. That is why the theory of analogies and anticipations suggested here is so different from humanistic theory. In the humanistic train of thought the analogies are the instrument by which to maintain, despite a fundamentally different Gegenstand, the methodological continuity of scientific thought in the various academic disciplines, while the anticipations represent the always progressive tendency of logical continuity, the scepter of sovereign thought.[5]

The humanistic conception therefore marks a radical break with sphere sovereignty,[6] while the analogies and anticipations of the Calvinist law-idea fully respect this sphere sovereignty.[7]

Every kind of take-over of other sovereign law-spheres by the sphere of science (scholarship) or by a personalistic philosophy of culture is precluded from the start by the principle of sphere sovereignty. Science has its own high value, but its range does not extend beyond its own sovereign sphere, where the true sovereign is not human reason but the divine legislator of ordinances for theoretical thought. Alongside it, and in organic coherence with it, we find all the other law-spheres in their integral sovereignty. Not a single sphere can replace or displace any other, for all sphere sovereignty is based in the cosmic plan of the supreme Sovereign of heaven and earth.

Furthermore, the Calvinist conception of the knowing subject likewise exhibits the sharp-etched lines of our law-idea.

Far from elevating reason as the logical creator of the Gegenstand (as in idealism), Calvinist epistemology proceeds from the view that all creatures can only be subject within the created law-spheres. Whenever we turn a certain Gegenstand into the object of our reflective thinking, it does not mean that the Gegenstand is not itself subject to various law-spheres rather than just being subject to the laws of our thought. It means, rather, that the knowing subject can get to know other subjects only by bringing to mind the coherence of subjectivity in which it is equally subject, jointly with the Gegenstand, to the laws that are grasped scientifically in the logical forms of relation and system.[8]

Analysis of the subject function (which alone is relevant when investigating a particular law-sphere) by abstracting it from the cosmic subject unity can never be anything other than a provisional analysis of what forms an unbreakable organic unity in God's cosmic plan.

Still another feature of the principle of sphere sovereignty needs to be pointed out with the greatest of emphasis.

Let us never forget that it is religion, the Christian awareness of God, that finds pregnant embodiment in the Calvinist law-idea. Hence, let us never reduce religion to a law-sphere next to others, since it underlies wholly, primarily, and universally, all sovereign spheres: namely, as a *passive* relation to God's creative and sustaining power in those law-spheres in which *unreasoning* nature serves God; and as an *active* relation to God in the law-spheres in which *rational* nature serves God.

Sin disrupted the active religious relation and cast man down into a state of enmity towards God and profound moral misery. But that relation was restored through the merit of Christ's death on the cross, and whenever that religious approach to life, possible only in Christ, was again accepted, religion revealed its universal regenerative power in that the creature in all areas of life lovingly bowed down again under God's ordinances, not as a slave before his master, but as a child of the Father who is in heaven.

God's work in the human heart is not bound to laws, and that is precisely why the Christian religion cannot be confined to a single law-sphere. Rather, it drives the born-again person out into the sinful world to join the battle everywhere for the maintenance of the divine ordinances and against the mania of the humanistic science ideal for abstraction, and to point again and again to the organic unity of all the law-spheres as it is expressed so gloriously in our law-idea.

CHAPTER 4

THE SIGNIFICANCE OF THE CALVINIST LAW-IDEA FOR THE SCIENCE OF LAW AND THE PHILOSOPY OF LAW

W HAT, NOW IS THE significance of the Calvinist law-idea for legal science as well as legal philosophy?

I believe its significance can be summarized in three interconnected values or functions of the law-idea.

(1) the heuristic value;

(2) the methodological value;

(3) the critical value in the service of the heuristic value.

(1) *The heuristic value of the Calvinist law-idea*

We have already come to know the heuristic value of the law-idea. Antithetically, it enables us to discover the various starting points of legal science and systems in legal philosophy, and to determine *in advance* what types of law-idea must lead to antinomies in jurisprudential and legal-philosophical thought.

The types of antinomies may be surveyed in advance by an analysis of the underlying law-idea. By reflection on the law-idea on which positivism is founded we can fathom this spiritual direction in its metaphysical character and predict the self-destruction of its positive ideal of knowledge. This way guides us in the discovery of the natural-law foundations of every legal theory that presents itself as positivistic, and in the determination of the nature of that masked natural law by checking it against the law-idea that underlies it. For without natural law no positivism on earth can exist at all.

(2) *The methodological value of the Calvinist-law-idea*

The methodological value of the Calvinist law-idea lies in the fact that it compels us to base scientific thought in general, and the science of law and legal philosophy in particular, on the principle of sphere sovereignty in its organic sense.

This will from the outset preclude from the science of law the rise of any naturalism, psychologism, logicism, sociologism, historicism, ethicism, and relativism.

The jural constitutes a sovereign law-sphere that is organically connected to all the other law-spheres. The science of law must therefore begin with the quality of the jural, the sovereign modality of the jural field of vision, by abstracting (analyzing) it from the organic-cosmic coherence of law spheres in order reflectively and intuitively to bring the meaning of this modality to consciousness.

In this jural modality the analogies of the modalities of the preceding law-spheres must be discovered.

The jural modality, and with it the entire legal sphere, is very complex in character; it is not one-dimensional, as the abstract neo-Kantian legal theory would have it, but it has as many dimensions as the number of analogies which the legal sphere can indicate.

As an illustration of the peculiar character of analogies in the legal sphere, consider the legal term *geldingstijd* (period of validity).[1] A time-bound period of validity undoubtedly rests on the substrate of natural time. But whereas natural time proceeds in one direction only, the jural analogy of time, peculiarly, can proceed in two directions (think of retroactive validity).

Therefore, the legal system may not be constructed in one continuous dimension, as Kelsen's school attempted to do, but it must follow the complicated structure of the jural modality and branch out into different dimensions. The jural modality itself is alone the common denominator under which the most diverse legal forms and figures must be subsumed in order to understand them in legal relations and in a legal system.

We are now also in a position to discover a moment of truth in all humanistic one-sidedness. Where the legal system was characterized by the mathematical-logical schools in humanistic legal theory as a "geometry of legal phenomena" (Kelsen), there law, by means of a logical analogy, is subjected to the mathematical methodology.

The Calvinist principle of sphere sovereignty opposes this for good reason. Yet the mathematical analogy can indeed be indicated as a meta-logical analogy of the idea of law in the jural modality. The problem of unity-in-diversity maintains itself as a mathematical analogy in the scope of the jural and is here founded on a mathematical substrate.[1a]

But in this field of vision this problem functions only as a legal problem, a problem determined by the normative jural modality. The majority principle, the problem of the unity of the state, of legal personality as the unity of many wills—evidently, they do all reside for one part within the mathematical analogies of the jural, yet they can never be approached by the mathematical concept of function.[2]

In the final analysis it is the jural itself that establishes the bond of unity among the many individuals.

When the psychological school of legal theory tries to understand the law as a psychological will, it no doubts violates the principle of sphere sovereignty and must necessarily embroil itself in antinomies. And yet, the fact that the legal sphere does show psychological analogies is certainly not in question. The jural will can never be a function of the norm, as the *Normlogik* school would have it. It is undoubtedly founded on a psychological substrate and lies in the sphere of the psychological analogies of the jural. But it is the jural modality which, ultimately, impresses its character on the jural will, and places it in the relation of attribution to the legal norm.

Remark: Siegfried Marck likewise, in his important study *Substanzbegriff und Funktions-begriff in der Rechtsphilosophie* (1925), attempted once again to restore the substantial element in the concepts of legal personality,

jural will, and the state. Marck was reacting to the functionalistic "Norm-Logic" that aims at resolving all substantial elements within the jural sphere into functions.
The direction he took, however, again leads directly into
the antinomy of the dialectical thought that flows from
the basic structure of the humanistic law-idea. By connecting with the "I-philosophy" of modern phenomenology and with cognitive psychology, Marck attempted
to save the substantial element in the categories of legal
personality and jural will by placing them in a necessary
relation to the total I of the living, real personality (p.
116). This "I" itself is then not a "unique experience"
or a relation, but a "center of experience" that is found
behind all psychological relations as the "condition of
their being conceived" (p. 89). This "I" concept exhibits
a *dialectical* character. Across the board his analysis is antinomic (compare Kant's paralogism of rational psychology!). It is the dialectical "synthesis" of all contradictions
created by psychological analysis. The psychological "I"
and the legal subject are not connected as substance and
relation, for in the legal subject one must observe the
genesis of an artificial "I" in its specific psychological
functional sense. For the jurally relevant action is not
taken up in the total stream of consciousness, but has
acquired an isolated, artificial, and rigid significance. The
legal person is a reification of the authentic real "I" (pp.
113–114). In this way Marck indeed wants to link up
with the former purely sociological concept of the power
and dominion of the state with a jural meaning. It is not
intended as a fundamental element in the concept of the

state, but in the determination of the task the state has as the all-inclusive totality of legal partners in subjection to the legal order. It is, namely, an essential task of each societal collectivity (*verband*) to respect its own collective norms and as it were *to live*. To that end the citizenry, as the power for maintaining the law, must organize itself (p. 145). The distinction between public law and private law, too, could thus be maintained—even if not in a formal sense, then certainly in respect of the sphere of the material contents of law (p. 146).

In opposition to this entire exposition, the same objections must be raised, on principle, that could be brought forward against all forms of humanistic thought insofar as the latter does not respect sphere sovereignty. By necessity it leads to antinomies. How is it possible, without facing the danger of antinomies, to save the substantial element in a legal personality through a theoretical relation to the functional "I-ness" of modern Act Psychology?

And how is it possible to save the sociological concept of a societal collectivity (*verband*) and power concept within the jural sphere through a relation to the purpose of the state?

Marck continues to adhere to the neo-Kantian "critical" standpoint according to which the form and the content of law must be strictly separated. In the thought of Marck the connection between the jural sphere and the surrounding spheres can never be maintained in a *formal* sphere but only within the *material* domain of law. But by doing this Marck entangles himself in the well-known antinomies of the form-content problem that we were compelled to point out with respect of the entire neo-Kantian legal theory. Whoever accepts the *Calvinist law-idea* must acknowledge this *complexity* in the jural modality itself and uncover in it the analogies of the surrounding law-spheres.

[End of Remark]

When the sociological school of political theory seeks to dissolve legal institutions (like state, municipality, province, association, etc.) into purely sociological relations, it undoubtedly violates the principle of sphere sovereignty and can only get stuck in antinomies. But it is beyond doubt that laws are largely based on social substrates and do contain an entire sphere of social analogies without which state, municipality and provinces can simply not be jurally understood. The legal distinction in private law, for example, between association and partnership is undoubtedly founded on a sociological substrate.[3]

In the final analysis, however, it is the jural modality that determines the jural character of all these communal relations.

When sociological political theory transforms the legal authority of government into a sociological concept of *Herrschaft* or power, then it undoubtedly violates the principle of sphere sovereignty and must necessarily embroil itself in antinomies. But again, it is beyond doubt that governmental authority rests on a sociological substrate of power and lies embedded in the sociological analogies of the jural.

Only, governmental authority is not sociological power and cannot be understood as a precarious, unfounded relation between sociological power and ethical task. It is the jural itself in which authority is ultimately founded.[4]

And so we could go on. We can point to the ethical anticipations and psychological analogies in the legal sphere, without which forms of guilt and "incriminating circumstances" cannot be properly distinguished in criminal law. However, ultimately it is the jural itself which, in its sovereign sphere, impresses its jural character on the forms of guilt (culpability).

Similarly, the important function of the economic analogies of the jural should be pointed out as based on the substrate of the economic law-sphere. All of property law, commercial law, as well as numerous other components of positive law, fall within these analogies. Concepts like "restitution for damages and interests," "usufruct," "usury," etc., cannot be understood jurally without reference to the economic law-sphere. However, here too, it is ultimately the jural that impresses its distinctive character on these concepts in the legal sphere.

A brief comment is in order about the notorious problem of the relation of *form* and *content* in the law. We will never be able to join Kelsen's norm-logical school in excluding the content of the law from the *reine Rechtslehre* as the goal of law. Form and content belong inseparably together. Whoever divorces legal content from legal form will not be left with a sociological, an economic, or a natural content, but with a hollow term, with nonsense. The form of law, furthermore, is by no means a creation of our consciousness: it is the sovereign divine modality of the jural sphere, which delimits its own sphere of modal categories (legal authority, legal subject, legal object, imputation, guilt, punishment, etc.).

The so-called legal content of positive law, however, is based on the political analogies in the jural, on the jural sediment of political law-formation. It follows that positive law must be understood as a teleological structure whose *meaning* needs to be investigated. But again, we must reject the position of Jhering and modern "*Interessen-jurisprudenz*" (the legal science of interests) which seeks to relativize law as a "*Zweck-relation*" (goal-relation). The means-end relation must always be founded in the jural modality itself; it must be determined by the jural itself, else the concept of law is destroyed, leading to insoluble antinomies.

For Calvinists, the science of law must, obviously, be built on a foundation of *natural law*. It seeks to anchor human legislation as well as customary law (common law and jurist-law) in divine jural ordinances. Absent that foundation, and the problems of legal authority, of the normative meaning of law, of imputation, of guilt and punishment will remain entangled in a web of antinomies.

As the foundation of positive law, Calvinism seeks not only a formal natural law (the so-called concept of law and its categories) but also material natural law (the material theory of the essence of law). In judicial institutions it seeks not only legal relations but also the divine nature of their essence. And as it does so in line with the Calvinist law-idea, it will also track down the substrates in which these institutions are organically connected with other law-spheres.[5]

However, not a single legal institution may be crystallized, in defiance of all historical development, into a rigid given. On the contrary, we profess that the material legal institutions come and go, continually adapting themselves to developments in other law-spheres.

The theory of authority, one of the fundamental problems of primary natural law, must also, in this sense, be based on the firm footing of the Calvinist law-idea. Neither the personalism and the historicism of Stahl's theory of legitimacy, nor the absolutization of power in sociological political theory, are acceptable to Calvinism. The view of authority in Reformed ecclesiology, with its emphasis on the legal character of authority exercised by duly elected office-bearers, and the republican feature of early Calvinism's view of government is pervaded by one and the same basic idea, ultimately founded in the Calvinist law-idea.[6]

And it was Calvin in particular, who, over against the humanistic mechanization of the institution of authority, once again emphatically referred to the organic character of the institution of the state, to the cosmic coherence with the other spheres of life.

> **Remark:** This also explains Calvin's defense of a legal and institutional basis for governmental authority; see his sermons on 1 Sam. 8 and 10 in *Corpus Reformatorum,* vol. 57: 554–555, 536–537:

In short, as peoples ought to be subject to their kings, so in their turn kings ought to obey and be submissive to the laws, so that they do not persuade themselves that anything is allowed, but instead turn all their counsels to the advantage of their subjects. . . .

. . . But here mention is made of the law of kingship, to demonstrate the mutual obligation between king and people, and vice versa. From this passage [namely 1 Sam. 10:25] we must therefore observe that Samuel, following the choice of Saul overseen by God himself, explained the main point and duty of Saul's calling and how he was to rule so as to protect and promote the worship of God and ensuring what is advantageous and useful to the entire people. But on the other hand, he explained to the people their duty toward the king, namely their obedience to the king, so that if the king should conscript a military force, impose a tax, and do similar things, they would know that they owed him obedience in all these things. Indeed from this passage we learn that all legitimate administration of the state is based on laws, and that therefore it is not enough that there be many men of outstanding authority, but that what is most necessary is that there be secure laws, whereby through a kind of bridle everyone be held to his duty, and that those who are seated at the helm of the state should not think that anything is permitted to them and accordingly allow themselves to transgress their limits.

And on the other hand, let the people be held to their duty, and let them know that they must not undertake anything senseless, nor rise up against their superiors, but let them be ruled by laws and statutes, and let everyone perform his duty in his own calling. Thus what ought to be noted here above all else is that all states of course are constituted by laws and ordinances. . . . For this reason we see that any state ought to be ruled by laws and decrees, whether a king reigns or public magistrates govern the state, in order that nothing be done according to anyone's whim, but that all learn from the laws what belong to their duty, and that they subject themselves and are submissive—and are as it were the armament of the people.

The Calvinist theory of authority at all times derived from the bond between governments and positive law, based upon a natural-law, divine foundation of right. This is illustrated in the following statement by Althusius (a figure largely neglected by humanistic historians). In his famous work, *Politica* (1610), chap. IX, he launches a serious polemic against Bodin's humanistic principle "*princeps legibus solutus est*" (the prince is above the law):

> The one who is said to have supreme power, should he subordinate his imperium and high office to civil law? Bodin *cum suis* say no. In their judgment there is a supreme power above civil law and not limited by it. I cannot agree with this. *For to liberate power from civil law is to release it to some extent from the bonds of natural and divine law. No civil law is possible if it does not have something of immutable equity, natural and divine, mixed in with it.* If it departs in any way from the standards of natural and divine law, it is not to be called "law" but is altogether unworthy of the name. (IX.21) (ital. added)

Here we see the practical jural significance of the Calvinist conception of divine sovereignty. That Althusius understood this fundamental, principled line of thought should have warned Gierke not to characterize him as a direct forerunner of Rousseau.

For that matter, anyone who analysed this impressive system of Althusius without bias and in terms of the law-idea underlying it, would recognize it as an elaboration (albeit not pure in all respects) of Calvinism's basic conception. Granted, Althusius (and with him, other Calvinist *monarchomachs* like Beza, Hotman, Du Plessis Mornay, Milton), in accordance with the spirit of the time, took the prevailing rights of the estates of the realm under feudal law and expanded them to become a principle of authority based on natural law (though with an appeal to positive constitutional law). Yet at the same time these writers, especially Althusius, opposed the revolutionary concept of popular sovereignty and taught that the *populus* is subject to positive law:

> We must now define this supreme power. We attribute it by right of sovereignty to the associated political body, which claims it for itself alone. . . . Universal power is called pre-eminent, primary, and supreme, *not because it is above the law, or absolute,* but, with respect to particular and special subordinate power that depends upon it, arises and flows from it, returns in time to it, and is furthermore bound to definite places. (IX, 21)

Authority is inherent in the organic state community, not in the atomistic popular masses. In the Preface to his *Politica* Althusius states:

Many jurists and politicians ascribe the rights of sovereignty to the prince and supreme magistrate. . . . I maintain the exact opposite, namely, that these rights of sovereignty, as they are called, are proper to the realm [i.e., the "universal symbiotic community"] to such a degree that they belong to it alone, and that they are the vital spirit, soul, heart, and life by which . . . the commonwealth lives, and without which it crumbles and dies.

The extent to which Althusius was opposed to a revolutionary democracy is as clear as daylight from his views expressed in *Politica*, chapter XXIII:

That is why the people is turbulent, mutinous, desirous of revolution, loathing the status quo, seeking an alternative order and condition of the state, averse to tranquility and a quiet life, especially when there is a [harsh] prince. (XXIII.7)

Hence the people is fierce, capricious, indomitable, and intolerant of servitude, and like a fierce bronc is to be managed by the same skill. (XXIII.5)

Furthermore, Althusius' entire *"pactum"* construction of social life is simply the jural superstructure on top of an organic-sociological substructure (cf. his *"symbiosis"* concept as he gradually unfolds his views). The institution of authority is for him an eternal divine ordinance. He does not construe it, mathematically as it were, by means of a contract between individuals:

It is a general and permanent law that in every association and species of symbiosis, some persons are rulers (chiefs, superintendents, prefects) or superiors, while others are subjects or inferiors. (*Politica*, I.11) When God, who is Lord of all, created the world, He prescribed for all creatures, even for trees, springs, rivers, and other created things, unique and distinct rules appropriate to their kind. (XVIII.21)

In this way, too, Althusius' theory of the [role of] "lower magistrates" or "ephors," a theory he borrowed from Calvin, stands in irreconcilable opposition to humanism's atomistic theory of popular sovereignty; cf. Chapter XVIII, "De Ephoris eorumque officio." He refers constantly to the organic structure of the authoritative institute, just as the very basis of his scientific method is anchored in the organic law-idea. Again, see the Preface to his *Politica*:

> I found it difficult to separate jural matters from political science. For as close as the relationship is of ethics with theology, or of physics with medicine, so close is the relationship of politics with jurisprudence. Where the moralist leaves off, there the theologian begins; where the physicist ends, the physician begins; where the political scientist ceases, the jurist takes over. . . . We must not leap readily across boundaries and limits [but] constantly observe the natural and true goal and form of each art, attending most carefully to them, lest we exceed the limits that justice lays down for each art . . . *In practice, however, no one denies that all the disciplines are connected*" (ital. added).

Note that here the theoretical view of sphere sovereignty is accepted upon an organic basis, even though this principle is not yet thought through in an epistemo-logical sense.

In due time I intend to analyze the theory of author-ity in more detail in my series of articles on "In den strijd om een Christelijke Staatkunde" in the journal *Antirev-olutionaire Staatkunde* of 1924–1927 ([Eng. trans., *The Struggle for a Christian Politics*].

See also the study of Professor Josef Bohatec, "De organische idee in de gedachten-wereld van Calvijn," as well as his important study, "Calvin's Vorsehungslehre" in *Calvinstudien: Festschrift zum 400. Geburtstage Johann Calvins* (1909).

[End of Remark]

Governmental authority derives its basis of validity from the same divine jural ordinances on which the validity of positive legal norms is based. It is the authority of an official within the legal order, and it is not based on a personal will but on the sovereign order of God. That is why both the maxim *princeps legibus solutus est* (a ruler is not bound by the laws), and the modern humanist theory of legal sover-eignty amounts to the negation of all jural sovereignty, two positions that are therefore completely at odds with the Cal-vinist conception of authority. And no less at odds with the fundamental idea of the Calvinist theory of government is the ethical-personalistic view of authority, while so-called legal positivism, which denies an independent authority of office (official authority) and only maintains an authority of positive law itself, cannot but destroy itself for lack of a deeper foundation for the normative character of its validity. This positivism is then compelled once again to resort to an agency outside positive law—whether that be the logic of sovereign thought (Kelsen), legal consciousness or the sense of justice (Krabbe), or legal sensitivity (Duguit). But in so doing it violates the principle of sphere sovereignty as well as its own fundamental positivist dogma, ensnaring it unavoidably in all sorts of antinomies.

In its theory of authority, too, Calvinism maintains sphere sovereignty, and in its conception of the *analogies of the law-idea* it guarantees the organic coherence with the spheres positioned round about the jural law-sphere.

All this belongs to the field of *primary natural law*, in which all positive law is based *qua talis*. Organically bound to the primary natural law is the so-called *political natural law* which norms the formation of law politically. The political *analogies* of positive law refer to it.

In this political natural law, the *material analogical legal quality* of law expresses itself, *by anticipation*, as *retribution*. Retribution is certainly not, as is commonly supposed, solely a category of criminal law. Rather, it is the universal meaning of all right law. But remember, this retribution too is not an abstract, one-dimensional category, not a *legal idea in a formal-logical sense*, but it must permeate all the analogies in its law-sphere, maintain in it the coherence with the other law-spheres, and in so doing, must realize itself in material legal principles that vary according to time and place. It is in this light that the so-called cultural and economic task of the state must be seen. There can be no cultural and no economic task of the state without a jural basis, without a foundation in political natural law. This is the password of sphere sovereignty as legal-political principle. Retribution is not the purpose of law, but the political-legal *meaning* of law. Every attempt to justify positive law by its purpose is based on a violation of sphere sovereignty, a relativization of the jural.

Calvinism, which on principle rejects every form of theodicy, can seek no other justification of positive law than the primary divine jural ordinances in which the validity of this law is based.

Special care must be taken not to confuse political natural law with ethics. Retribution and love can never be understood as two sides of the same coin. Any attempt to do so will result in insoluble antinomies, antinomies that are only seemingly resolved when ethics is denatured and seen as law, or law is denatured as ethics, or all law is radically rejected.

However, the legal-political principle of retribution does harbor ethical anticipations, making it incumbent upon the legislator to reckon with both the level of people's ethical convictions and the moral law of God.

Understandably, sphere sovereignty plays a very special role in political natural law. The formation of law, although bound to the other law-spheres in a myriad of ways, may never violate the sphere sovereignty of the other law-spheres.[7] The so-called general interest or common good has a politically acceptable meaning only when it is primarily based in the principle of retribution and is secondarily limited by the sovereignty of the other law-spheres. State absolutism is the political wisdom of the humanist ideal of continuity. Calvin-ist natural law confronts this human wisdom with the divine wisdom of sphere sovereignty.

(3) *The critical value of the Calvinist law-idea in the service of its heuristic value*

Our brief discussion of the meaning of political natural law takes us naturally to a consideration of our law-idea's *critical value*.

It consists in this, that from the indissoluble, harmoni-ous coherence of all the law-spheres and, flowing from it, the *rejection, on principle, of antinomy*, we may conclude that no law-sphere can come into conflict with another law-sphere so long as one takes the divine ordinances of every sphere as the norm for all our action. This is the critical value of our law-idea. The jural sphere appeals and refers to all the law-spheres positioned round about it in the cosmic coherence, and the laws of all these spheres bolster and buttress each other. This insight is of enormous value, also for the theory of the formation of law. When positive law comes into con-flict with the ethical ordinances of God, or with economic laws, or with historical laws of development, then our law-idea teaches us that those conflicts do not stem from the divine essence of the jural, but instead have been elicited by the legislator's neglect of sovereign limits, by a violation of the principle of sphere sovereignty, or by an incorrect appli-cation of political natural law, for example by not reckon-ing with developments within substrates of the jural sphere. Then the broken harmony must be restored, and any wrong elements must be removed from positive law. But the jural law-sphere's own proper independence may never be violated, as occurs in ethical personalism, nor may we assume a fundamental conflict between law and love, as occurs in the Christian sects.

Furthermore, the Calvinist law-idea provides us with the critical insight that in the long run lawmakers, when they continually transgress the boundaries, can do nothing against sphere sovereignty except to create chaos instead of a legal order.

The legal philosophy of Max Ernst Mayer assigns a critical function to legal norms with respect to conventional and other cultural norms. Thus, law is given a critical function with respect to culture by separating the culturally valuable from the cultural worthless by means of a jural sieve.[8]

This cultural-philosophical conception, which ultimately acknowledges no higher criterion for the law than the ethical idea of humanity, in a certain sense sees matters the wrong way around. For the critical task here assigned to the law cannot be carried out by the law in its own strength. That task belongs only and exclusively, by virtue of its sovereign significance, to the law-idea, which, in the organic-harmonious idea of sphere sovereignty, subjects all human establishment of norms to the test of the divine ordinances, ordinances that bolster and buttress each other in mutual coherence.

This then is what I wished to convey to you about the significance of the law-idea for the science of law and the philosophy of law. My thetical exposition could not, in the time available, be more than a program, but this program, once and for all, bears the imprint of the Calvinist law-idea.

Anyone who has ever probed the depths of this law-idea, anyone who is open to Calvinism's heroic strength of faith and the captivating, life-embracing, soul-fortifying vitality of its law-idea, anyone who has come to know the joy of burning zeal for God and his kingdom and has seen the entire world in its sin and misery and the area of scholarship as a bulwark where faith must plant the victory sign of divine sovereignty, such a one can no longer make a pact with the wisdom of this world. Restlessly, roused as by a divine compulsion, he pursues a new purpose, unheard of in its greatness, in the light of which all temporal ideals grow dim: namely, to convince the whole world that God, the Lord, is King of heaven and earth, also the King of our scholarship.

To Thee, then, Lord my God, I direct my prayer in this hour. [1] To thank Thee for Thy wondrous leading in my life, to thank Thee for every trial and every chastisement, to thank Thee that Thou hast now called me to serve Thee in this university.

Inspire my work at this university and grant that Thy strength be made perfect in my weakness. Grant, O Father of all mercy, that love for Thee and the expansion of Thy kingdom may continue to burn in my heart, and that my steps may never deviate from the way of truth which Thou hast revealed to us in Thy holy Son.

And as our weak powers fall short, as our heart is always inclined towards sin, worldliness and faint-heartedness, wilt Thou, holy Father, confirm Thy kingdom in our academic work and use it to disrupt, also there, the kingdom of the lie, so that through Thy Spirit our work as human beings may be sanctified.

Curators and Directors of this University,

You have entrusted me with the highly responsible position of professor in which I am now placed at this University. I am grateful to you for the confidence placed in me and hope to conduct myself worthy of that confidence. That you, in various respects, have graciously accommodated my desire not to abrogate my relationship with my former vocation entirely only increases my sense of gratitude. When, following much internal struggle, I finally had the courage to comply with your wish, it was not a decision taken in my own strength, but a deed done in the awareness that God has now called me to this task. This freed me from faintheartedness and personal preference, so that I could place the future into God's hands with childlike trust. In these times of serious difficulties in our own circles relying on human strength will not avail, but what will help is to know that in the exercise of our task we are supported by the quiet prayer of so many thousands of our people who love this university. As long as this thousandfold prayer for our university will continue to go up, as long as the faith of our entire people will carry this university, so long it cannot go under.

It is for me a deeply distressing thought that I must now take the place of a man whose premature and tragic death has robbed the law faculty of one of its most outstanding members.[4] Professor Zevenbergen's winsome personality, the enormous amount of work that he carried out at this university and that promised so much for the future, his selfless zeal for work—all of this will live on in our memory as an example of character and scrupulous devotion to duty. The thought that I would have to take over this task, albeit in part, from a man endowed with such great intellectual gifts was not the least of my thoughts that more than once filled me with trepidation. The more so since I could certainly not appeal to the motto *"In magnis et voluisse sat est."*[5] Of the disciplines entrusted to my care it is especially legal philosophy and the encyclopedia of the science of law that are most demanding of one's scholarly discernment and faithfulness to first principles.

If on the other hand I consider the goal, then I accept this task with joy, in the awareness that especially in these areas the light will shine on the depths of that world and life view to which I know myself attached with heartfelt love for life.

Members of the Law Faculty,

It was your desire to have me as the successor to Zevenbergen, and I am most grateful to you, who have been my teachers[6] and to whom I already owe so much, that you have given me such the warm reception in your midst. It makes me look forward to pleasant, collegial collaboration. Lacking experience, I will frequently call on you for guidance and information, but I am convinced that you will gladly support me with your great knowledge and mature insight.

The disciplines which I am to teach[7] will mostly require

continuous contact with fields you have mastered; legal philosophy especially, it seems to me, cannot be fruitfully treated without continually consulting concrete legal material. I shall always count it a special privilege to be able to count on your counsel and instruction and in that discern a proof of your collegial sentiments towards me, and of a unity of spirit that binds us together in the interest of a common cause.

Members of the Faculty,

I commend myself to the friendship and kindness of you all, to support me with your expertise and ability. Where the philosophical part of my task will continually put me in touch with the disciplines positioned round about the science of law, I shall frequently call on you as well for information and advice. It is a wonderful thought for me that simultaneously with my appointment a man has been called to this university to whom I am attached not only by family ties but even more intimately by bonds of many years of friendship and intellectual kinship. That you, Dr. Vollenhoven, will now occupy the chair of philosophy at this university assures me not only of daily collaboration and refreshing interaction, but also, and this I consider even more important, of close affinity between each other's teaching along the lines of thinking that we share.[8] In the common field we shall be working in, you will be of inestimable support to me.

Esteemed Fabius,

In this hour I feel the need to remember you, my teacher, who have devoted the best years of your life to this university. Your interest in the course of my life and in my work never flagged, and when I faced difficult decisions you were always there for me with helpful advice. In the challenging time that now awaits me I shall continue to count on your support and friendship, especially in providing information for fulfilling a task in the Law Faculty that is only a small part of the responsibilities that once rested on your shoulders.[9]

Members of the Board of the Dr. Abraham Kuyper Institute,

It is not without feelings of melancholy that I am about to relinquish an important part of the task with which you entrusted me at the Kuyper Institute, and which had grown dear to me as my life's calling. I take comfort in the knowledge that I need not sever all ties with the Institute but will be able to maintain contact with it also in the future. Rest assured that I shall also henceforth neglect to do nothing that is within my power for the advancement of its wonderful purpose and to win increasing support for it.

Dear Mother,

In this hour, the thoughts of both of us reach out to him whose dearest wish it was that I should follow in his footsteps and devote my life to the service of the God Who in all trials was a mighty fortress of his faith.

That desire has now come to fulfillment in a special way, but he himself was not permitted to see any of it. That you are now present here and that I am able to convey my gratitude to both of you fills and moves me with thankfulness.

Ladies and Gentlemen of the Student Body,

It is with particular warmth that I speak to you, who will now be my students. I ask for your love, your passionate heart, for the great task that awaits us.

I come to you with confidence; you will not disappoint me. For the ideal that fills my entire soul is alive in you as well: to permeate our scholarship throughout with the spirit of our holy principles!

Who is there among you that would demur and lag behind when the King of our scholarship summons us to the battle of the spirits? In particular I would like to call your attention at this time to legal philosophy, even though—indeed, because—it is not a compulsory course. For it is there that the foundations of our world and life view first reveal themselves; above all, it is there that we must systematically build upon these foundations. And there especially I shall repeatedly have to remind you that scholarship demands that you not spare yourselves the effort of independent thought by easily accepting what others have already thought before you, but instead, through strenuous sifting and evaluating, to learn to distinguish the worthwhile from the worthless. I have no desire to impose my own subjective opinion on you, but I want to pass on to you a pure and true touchstone, to try and provide you with a clearer awareness of the firm foundations of your world and life view.

Never forget that the requirement of science comes to you not as a requirement of human culture but as a divine requirement of Christ your King, who assigned the field of scholarship to you to work in.

Not everyone is able to do original work in this field. But those among you who have received the talents to contribute, however little, to deepening and enriching our knowledge in this area, those among you who have heard God's call to serve Him in this special area, will be guilty of sinfully shirking your responsibility if this call does not elicit a positive response on your part, and your talents are not readily placed at the service of your King, Who not only claims your mind, but Who also has a claim, solely and sovereignly, on your entire life.

In view of the legacy left to us in the impressive intellectual achievements gained through hard labor by Calvinist thinkers also in modern times, it behooves us to devote ourselves with ardor and exert ourselves with enthusiasm, while using all our strength and might, to appropriate that work and, if possible, according to the measure of our talents, to enlarge upon it, in the spirit of the words of the poet:

> *Was du ererbt von deinen Vätern hast*
> *erwirb es, um es zu besitzen!*[10]

I thank you.

NOTES

[1] This statement comes from Thomas Hobbes, as found in the "Dedicatory Epistle" to his *De Corpore politico, or Elements of the law, moral & politik* (London, 1650). Before long I hope to publish in the journal *Anti-Revolutionaire Staatkunde* an analysis of Hobbes' natural law in the light of the law-idea of humanism, under the title "In den strijd om een Christelijke Staatkunde: Proeve eener fundeering der Calvinistische levens- en wereldbeschouwing in hare wetsidee." [Eng. trans., *The Struggle for a Christian Politics: An Essay in Grounding the Calvinistic Worldview in Its Law-Idea* (2008).]

[2] The humanistic science ideal clearly shows the influence of the Platonic concept of science (*hypothesis, logon didonai, ta phainomena diasõzein*) and is suffused with both a Diocretian and a pantheistic spirit.

[2a] The quotation is from Goethe's poem, *The Sorcerer's Apprentice*, line 91.

[3] Wilhelm Dilthey, "Das Wesen der Philosophie," in Paul Hinneberg, *Die Kultur der Gegenwart* (1905), I, 62 (ital. added).

[4] Cf. Ernst Cassirer, *Das Erkenntnisproblem in die Philosophie und Wissenschaft der neueren Zeit* [The problem of knowledge in modern philosophy and science] (1922), II, 189–90: "Even Leibniz' concept of God, when completed,

ends up in this thought: God is nothing but a "rational belief in the internal agreement between the 'realm of nature' and the 'realm of goals.'" The equation, *Universal harmony, that is God*, constitutes, long before the actual monadology is conceived, the point of departure for Leibniz' metaphysics. At the same time it remains the target that the manifold schools of research point to and aim at." Very much to the point is Cassirer's comment on p. 189: "The abstract mathematical concept of *function* is widened into the concept of harmony for ethics and metaphysics. That which earlier seemed to be an irreconcilable contrast to the mathematical, natural scientific mode of observation, now appears as an expansion and an ideal conclusion."

See also Albert Görland, "Der Gottesbegriff bei Leibniz" [The concept of God in Leibniz], *Philosophischen Arbeiten*, ed. by H. Cohen and P. Natorp (1907).

We know how J. G. Herder in his *Ideen zu einer Philosophie der Geschichte der Menschheit* [Outline of a philosophical history of mankind], 4 vols. (1784–91) applied this Leibnizian idea of continuity in order to have his humanistic ideal function in history as the highest stage of nature.

[5] Immanuel Kant, *Kritik der reinen Vernunft* (Groszherzog Wilhelm Ernst ed., 1922), pp. 406ff.: "The antinomy of pure reason restricts the number of possible antinomies to four and develops them in terms of four cosmological ideas of reason which in turn are correlated with the four titles of the categories of understanding, namely: (I) "The absolute completeness of the *composition* of the given totality of all phenomena"; (II) "The absolute completeness of the *di-*

176

vision of a given phenomenal totality"; (III) "The absolute completeness of the *origination* of an appearance as such"; and (IV) "The absolute completeness of the dependence of the existence of the changeable in its phenomenal appearance" (p. 443)]. Next to these antinomies, in which those of practical reason are already implied, Kant also knows the antinomies of the "*aesthetischen Urteilskraft*" (the aesthetic judgment)," developed in the dialectic of "*der aesthetische Urteilskraft*" and the antinomies of "*der teleologischen Urteilskraft*" (the teleological judgment), which are likewise developed in a critical dialectical way.

[6] See Kant's *Kritik der Urteilskraft* (same ed.) VI, 19:

Whether or not there be an unbridgeable gulf between the domain of the concept of nature (the sensory) and the domain of the concept of freedom (the super–sensory), so that no transition is possible from the former to the latter (i.e., through the theoretical use of reason)—as though there were two different worlds, where the former has no influence on the latter—nevertheless, whatever the case may be, the latter *ought* to have an influence on the former: the concept of freedom ought to be realized in the world of the senses by means of the purpose that was assigned to it by its laws. Consequently, we are to think of nature in such a way that at least the form of its law–conformity allows for the possibility of realizing the purposes according to the laws of freedom. There must therefore be a ground for the *unity* of the super-sensory (which lies at the basis of nature) with that which is practically contained in the concept of freedom; and the concept of this ground, regardless *whether it arrives at its cognition in either a theoretical or practical way, hence has no domain of its own,* nonetheless makes possible the transition from the mode of thinking according to the principles of the one toward the mode of thinking according to the principles of the other. (ital. added)

From this we see how the teleological principle in Kant is unable to delimit a knowledge domain with an independent foundation.

[7] See *Kritik der Urteilskraft*, pp. 43ff., a passage in Kant's Introduction that deals with the "Verknüpfung der Gesetzgebungen des Verstandes und der Vernunft durch die Urteilskraft" [the nexus between the laws imposed by the understanding and those imposed by reason through the judgment]. The *Kritik der Urteilskraft* poses the problem of the organic specification, of individuality, but only as *a transitional problem for knowledge about causal law–conformity.* Cf. pp. 31–32: "The capacity to judge also contains an *a priori* principle for the possibility of nature, albeit only in a subjective respect, whereby we do not prescribe a law to nature (as autonomy) but a law to ourselves (as heteronomy), a law for our reflection on nature—a law that one can call *the law of the specification of nature* in respect of its empirical laws. . . . For it is not a principle of the determining capacity but merely of the reflecting capacity to judge. Our sole aim is that, in whatever way nature chooses to organize itself by its general laws, we should aim to investigate its empirical

laws in accordance with that principle and the maxims based on it. *For it is only so long as that holds that we can make any headway with the use of our understanding in our experience and our acquisition of knowledge.*" (ital. added)

See also *Kritik der teleologischen Urteilskraft*, p. 330. Frequently Kant searches for a foundation of the deeper—for us unknowable—unity between *telos* and *causa*, in the super-sensory substrate of nature, the "thing-in-itself." But in Kant's critical idealism alone, which, according to the proper assessment of Nicolai Hartmann, already exceeds a "maximum of metaphysics," this metaphysical idea continues to hover in the air.

[8] As Georg Lasson correctly remarks in his edition of Hegel's *Encyclopaedie* (Leipzig: Meiner, 1923), p. xxii, Fichte's identity philosophy remains stuck in subjective *pathos*, which groans under the tyranny of the object and liberates itself again by way of asceticism. The I does not know what to do with the non-I except to defend itself against the non-I and to maintain itself as being different from the non-I.

This also explains why Fichte, in his view of law and the state, remained stuck for such a long period in an individualistic personalism—a view according to which the state and legal institutions are only passing phases, to be conquered by the free, ethical personality. The antinomy between legal coercion and moral freedom, created by the identity postulate of the humanistic personality ideal, had to make its effect felt within subjective idealism. Only later, when Fichte experiences the awakening of a national consciousness, does he appreciate the moral value and task of the national state; see his

Reden an die Deutsche Nation [Address to the German Nation]. But in his later development Fichte makes a transition from subjective idealism to a religiously absolute idealism. This altered standpoint already clearly comes to light in his philosophy of history which he developed in his *Grundzügen des gegenwärtigen Zeitalters* [Fundamentals of the Contemporary Age]. From this point on, Fichte again attempts to provide rest for the infinite restless activity in an absolute *being*—which is for him the Godhead, who creates in eternal rest its own copy (*Abbild*), absolute knowledge which now replaces the pure "theoretical I." And this image attempts to realize itself eternally in an infinite striving, which coincides with the "pure practical I." In this way Fichte clearly joined the neo–Spinozist movement. In connection with the development of Fichte's legal and political theory, cf. W. Metzger, *Gesellschaft, Recht und Staat in der Ethik des Deutschen Idealismus* [Society, law and state in the ethics of German idealism], (Heidelberg: Winter, 1917), pp. 199ff., esp. pp. 133ff.

[9] From Novalis we know the phrase: "Nature ought to become moral, we are its educator, . . . its moral stimulus."

[10] Typical for the a-nomic trend of the Romantic personality ideal are the words of Novalis: "Laws throughout contradict morality" and "Laws are the complement of deficient natures and beings." (Quoted in Metzger, op. cit., p. 207). What is here revived is the theory of the "universal man" or the all-round genius of the early Renaissance.

[11] A penetrating analysis of this inner dialectic, which could only drive thinkers from Kant to Hegel, is provided by

Richard Kroner in his *Von Kant bis Hegel,* 2 vols. (Tübingen, 1921, 1924). See also the review article by Erich Przywara, "Thomas oder Hegel," *Logos* 15.1 (1926), a study which does, however, suffer from the usual Roman Catholic misunderstanding of the spiritual meaning of the Reformation.

[12] This threefold dialectical development of the idea constitutes the whole of science. "Yet the Idea plainly shows itself as thought identical to itself and simultaneously as the activity itself, to be for itself, standing opposite itself, and in this other being to be only with itself." *Encyclopädie,* 2nd impr., p. 50. For Hegel, accordingly, science differentiates into three parts: 1. logic, as the science of the Idea "in–and–for–itself"; 2. nature philosophy, as the science of the Idea in its "being–other"; and 3. the philosophy of the Spirit, as the Idea which returns from its being–other to itself.

[13] Hegel elaborated the idea of *staatsraison* in his *Philosophie des Rechts* of 1821, §§ 336 and 337:

> Since states are related to one another as autonomous entities and so as particular wills on which the very validity of treaties depends, and since the particular will of the whole as to its content is simply a will for its own welfare alone, it follows that welfare is the highest law governing the relation of one state to another. This is all the more the case since the Idea of the state is precisely to overcome the clash between *right* (i.e., empty abstract freedom) and *welfare* (i.e., the particular content which fills that emptiness), and it is only when states become *concrete* wholes that they attain recognition.

The substantial welfare of the state is its welfare as a concrete state with its own specific interests and situation and its no less special foreign affairs, including its specific treaty relations. Its government therefore is a matter of particular wisdom, not of universal Providence. . . . Similarly, its aim in relation to other states and its principle for justifying wars and treaties is not a universal thought (the thought of philanthropy) but only its injured (or threatened) welfare as something specific and peculiar to itself.

More on Hegel's theory of the *staatsraison* in Meinecke, *Die Idee der Staatsräson* (1924), pp. 427ff. [Eng. trans., *Machiavellism: The Doctrine of Raison d'État and Its Place in Modern History* (1957), pp. 343–369.]

See also the excellent works by Franz Rosenzweig, *Hegel und der Staat,* vol. II (1920), pp. 173 ff., and by Hermann Heller, *Hegel und der nationale Machtstaatsgedanke im Deutschland* [Hegel and the national power state in Germany] (1921).

World history turns out to be the highest power above states: "*Die Weltgeschichte ist das Weltgericht*" [World history is the final judge]. Where only the real is rational, the present is judged in that it becomes the past: through ceasing to be real, it turns out to be abandoned by Reason.

Notes to Chapter 1
The Nature of Antinomy

[1] *General Editor's note*: Dooyeweerd employs the Dutch words *antinomie* in order to designate the (theoretical) attempt to *fuse* irreducible spheres of law or "law-spheres." When he uses the term *tegenstrijdigheid* in the same sense, it is incorrect to translate it as *contradiction*, since according to Dooyeweerd the latter term designates something *intra*-modal, appearing merely within the logical aspect. When the terms *antinomie* and *tegenstrijdigheid* are used interchangably, the latter term will be rendered as "a clash of laws."

[2] This view of the nature of an antinomy is already built entirely upon the Calvinistic law-idea with its sovereign law-spheres. Of course, whoever stands on the basis of the humanistic law-idea, in which at best only two sovereign spheres are acknowledged—those of *Sein* and *Sollen*, which actually cannot be genuine spheres—can only define the nature of antinomy differently. Kant's view of the antinomies of "pure reason" is entirely based upon his critical transcendental philosophy: here the antinomy arises by exceeding the boundaries of the understanding, the categories of which are confined to experience yet which cut themselves off from experience. On the other hand, the antinomy also arises by overstepping the limits of pure reason, which misuses its ideas as categories of the understanding. Concerning the genesis of this theory of antinomies in Kant's system, see

Carl Siegel, "Kant's antinomienlehre im Lichte der Inaugural Dissertation," *Kantstudien* 30.1/2 (1925): 67ff.

[3] See Max Ernst Mayer, s.v. *"Rechtsphilosophie,"* in *Encyclopädie der Rechts- und Staatswissenschaft*, Kohlrausch and Kaskel, eds. (1922), p. 87.

[4] Paul Natorp, *Die logischen Grundlagen der exakten Wissenschaften* [The logical foundations of the exact sciences], 2nd ed. (1921), p. 218: "But with that, it is stated that from now on there are no longer any conceptual barriers of whatever kind that cannot be crossed. Only the procedure itself of this justified border crossing can be called "absolute," in the sense that it is a match for every boundary that the sovereignty of thought might want to challenge.

[5] What we have in mind here are the antinomies of the modern set theory that functions in the thinking of some of its theoretical proponents as a multiplicity theory, with the pretention to be a part of a universal, pure logic. Among them are Dedekind, Schoenflies, Cantor, and from the angle of epistemology in particular Natorp in his earlier mentioned work *Die logischen Grundlagen der exakten Wissenschaften*; Cassirer in his *Substanzbegriff und Funktionsbegriff* [Substance concept and function concept] (1910)], pp. 31ff.; and Husserl in his *Ideen zu einer reinen Phänomenologie* [Ideas for a pure phenomenology] (1913), pp. 18, 276). To my mind these antinomies can be traced back to a leveling of the boundaries between the domains of logic, arithmetic, geometry, and mathematical physics (to which

belongs, I would contend, infinitesimal calculus).

For example, Cantor's theory of "transfinite sets"—whose subsets are "equivalent to them" [*Mathematische Annalen* 46 (1915): 495]—gets entangled in the antinomy of actual infinity already laid bare by Kant. By definition, it creates the antinomy between transfinity and the logical axiom *totum parte maius* (the whole is bigger than its parts). (Of course, we have no quarrel with the practical results of set theory, only with its epistemological foundation.)

Furthermore, consider the antinomies (called *paradoxes* by the theoreticians of set theory) in which certain theorems of set theory get entangled. Thus, for example, Cantor's theorem that Aleph-nul (ℵ), the smallest set of transfinite cardinal numbers, is not altered through the addition of or multiplication by a finite number or by being raised to the power of finite exponents.

Also think about the paradox of the "set of all sets," etc. In this connection, see Joseph Petzoldt, "Beseitigung der mengentheoretischen Paradoxa durch logisch einwandfreie Definition des Mengenbegriffs" [Sidestepping the paradoxes of set theory through an unobjectionable definition of the set concept], *Kantstudien* 30 (1925): 346ff.

An excellent analysis of these antinomies is found in the work of Theodor Ziehen, *Das Verhältnis der Logik zur Mengenlehre* [The relation of logic to set theory] (1917).

General Editor's note: Dooyeweerd eventually opted for the intuitionistic acceptance of the potential infinite only, rejecting altogether the idea of actual infinity (see *The Collected Works of Herman Dooyeweerd*, Series A, vols. I–IV (Lewiston,

NY: Edwin Melen Press), I, 98–99 note 1; II, 92, 340 note 1. That Dooyeweerd's theory of modal aspects indeed opens up the possibility to give fresh meaning to the potential and the actual infinite is argued by D. F. M. Strauss, "Philosophical Reflections on Continuity," *Acta Academica* 34.3 (2002): 1–32, where a distinction is drawn between the *successive infinite* and the *at once infinite*.

Notes to Chapter 2
Antinomies in Humanistic Legal Science

Notes to 2.1 The naturalistics types

[1] Alfred Vierkandt lists the following as unassailable truths discovered by modern sociology: 1. The subordination drive (discovered by Tarde and McDougall); 2. The basic societal relationships (Tönnies, Staudinger, Vierkandt); 3. The constant regularity of societal relationships (Stammler, Vierkandt); 4. The predominance of communal relations as regards the other basic relations (Vierkandt); 5. The extension of the self (self–consciousness) and self–awareness (McDougall and others); 6. The existence of objective social structures whose fluctuating individuals are merely the bearers—long known, of course, but still awaiting basic understanding; cf. A. Vierkandt, *Gesellschaftslehre. Hauptprobleme der Philosophischen Soziologie* [Theory of society: Main problems in philosophical sociology] (1923), p. 4.

As for the laws discovered by McDougall during the Second World War regarding the so-called higher group forms, see the recent work by J. J. von Schmid, *Staatsrechtsweten-schap en Sociologie* [The science of constitutional law and sociology] *(1926)*, pp. 29ff.

N.B. In the context of my own view, explained below, regarding the character of the science of law, sociological results such as these should of course be greatly appreciated for contributing to our knowledge of the "substrates of law" upon which the sociological analogies of the jural sphere are built.

[2] The chief publication of this school is the *Zeitschrift für vergleichende Rechtswissenschaft* [Journal for a comparative science of law], established in 1878. Typical for this entire orientation is the following statement by Albert Hermann Post: "There are specific laws according to which every organic configuration that is formed within the human race unfolds above the individuals; and these laws can be brought to light through a comparison of the corresponding developmental stages of all extant and extinct organisms belonging to a particular genus. Determining these laws will be the first task of any political and legal science in the future." *Der Ursprung des Rechts* [The origin of law] (1876), p. 7. See also by the same author: *Grundrisz der Ethnologischen Jurisprudenz* [Outline of an ethnological jurisprudence], 2 vols. (1894/95).

[3] The psychological school in the main is naturalistic in its orientation and therefore has countless points of contact with modern sociology. Most of its adherents are "*Freirecht-ler.*" Their research is aimed at providing explanations of legal phenomena by means of psychological experiments. Cf.

the paper read by Julius Ofner to the Vienna Bar Association, "Die naturwissenschaftliche Methode im Recht" [The natural-scientific method in law], as well his book *Das Experiment im Recht* [Experiments in Law] (1882). In addition, see Josef Kohler, "Die Erforschung des Rechtsbewusztseins durch Beobachtung und Experiment" [Studying legal awareness by means of observation and experiment], *Juristenblätter* 41 (1912).

Typical is the statement of the Viennese professor Helmut Bartsch, "Die Zukunft der Rechtswissenschaft" [The future of the science of law], *Archiv für Rechts- und Wirtschaftsphilosophie* 6 *(*1912/13): 127ff.: "Should this new school catch on, we may hope that the loneliness of jurists among other scholars would come to an end. Institutions would be created which would be able to determine legal phenomena similar to the way in which, for example, meteorological or chemical processes are determined" (p. 128).

See also Eugen Ehrlich, "Die Erforschung des lebenden Rechts [Studying living law]," *Schmoller's Jahrbücher* 35 (1911); and his "Ein Institut für lebendes Recht" [An Institute for living law], *Verhandlungen* des 31. Deutschen Juristen Tages, vol. II.

Franz Klein published the work, *Die psychischen Quellen des Rechtsgehorsams und der Rechtsgeltung* [The psychic sources of obedience to law and legal validity] (1912).

Another work is that of August Sturm, *Die psychologische Grundlage des Rechts. Ein Beitrag zur allgemeinen Rechtslehre* [The psychological basis of law: A contribution to the science of law] (1910).

⁴ Cf. esp. Hans Kelsen, *Hauptprobleme der Staatsrecht-slehre entwickelt aus der Lehre vom Rechtssatze* [Main problems of political theory, developed from the theory of legal propostions] (1910; 2nd impr., 1923), pp. 97ff., 145, 148ff.), in which he still continues the static position that he abandoned in 1920. See also his booklet, *Über Grenzen zwischen juristischer und soziologischer Methode* [The boundaries between the jural and sociological method] (1911), and his *Der soziologische und der juristische Staatsbegriff* [The sociological and juristic concept of the state] (1922), and his most recent work, *Allgemeine Staatslehre* [A general theory of the state] (1925), esp. pp. 3–25, 55–60, 61, 74 ff., 97 ff., et passim.

⁵ The reference is to the son of the famous founder of modern phenomenology, Gerhart Husserl. In his work, *Rechtskraft und Rechtsgeltung* [Legal force and legal validity] (1925), p. 93, we read: "Our thesis regarding the foundation of every right in an act of the will should not be understood as if the legal validity of every law promulgated by the jural community as a whole were dependent upon the factual acknowledgment of the totality of legal subjects belonging to this legal sphere. That is not so. A law that came into existence in a constitutional manner also holds for those citizens who did not participate in its coming into being and who now oppose it. It is not against their will, for in a normative sense these legal subjects in that law encounter their own will." Further on the same page: "Through the constitution, individuals empower other persons jurally to act on their behalf. The laws posited by these bearers of the will of the

individuals—for example the *Reichstage* [Imperial Diets]—were sanctioned in advance through an act of submission that holds for the constitution and all the legal consequences following from it. A thief who is sentenced to one year in prison sends his own will into prison. Through the organ of the court acting on behalf of him, this thief has sentenced himself. By stealing he deviated from the norm of his true will as citizens of the state."

This entire view entangles itself in an insoluble antinomy, for a little earlier the act of submission is portrayed as a purely psychological fact: "But the act of submission must be real; it must have been performed as a fact of the psychological will" (p. 72). See the appeal to Hobbes on pp. 75 and 76.

[6] Ernst Zitelmann, *Irrtum und Rechtsgeschäft. Eine psychologisch-juristische Untersuchung* [Error and legal action: A psychological-juristic investigation] (1879), p. 79; for his psychologistic method, see pp. 14ff.

[7] Zitelmann, *Irrtum und Rechtsgeschäft*, p. 238.

[8] W. Schuppe, "Der Begriff des Rechts," *Grünhuts Zeitschrift für das privat- und öffentliches Recht* 10 (1883): 356.

[9] Zitelmann, *Irrtum und Rechtsgeschäft*, pp. 201ff.

[10] Christoph Sigwart, *Kleine Schriften 2* (1897), p. 177.

[11] Zitelmann, *Irrtum und Rechtsgeschäft*, p. 18.

[12] Ibid., p. 19.

[13] Ibid. p. 20.

[14] G. Barnich, *Essai de politique positive basée sur l'énergétique sociale de Solvay* [Essay in positive politics on the basis of Solvay's social energetics] (1919), p. 72. Dr. Georges Barnich is the current Director of the Solvay Institute in Brussels.

[15] G. Ratzenhofer, *Soziologische Erkenntnis* [Sociological knowledge] (1898), pp. 25 ff. His monistic-naturalistic view of the world is further developed in his *Der positive Monismus und das einheitliche Princip aller Erscheinungen* (1899); *Positive Ethik: Die Verwirklichung des Sittlich-Seinsollenden* (1901); and *Die Kritik des Intellekts: Positive Erkenntnistheorie* (1902), all published with Brockhaus in Leipzig. Typical for this tendency of continuity of the humanistic science ideal is Ratzenhofer's statement in *Soziologische Erkenntnis*, p. 84, that the "social law" of "interdependence" is merely a modification of the force of gravity, while gravitational force in turn is a modification of the universal basic law of the "interdependence of all things."

[16] G. Ratzenhofer, *Wesen und Zweck der Politik als Theil der Sociologie und Grundlage der Staatswissenschaften* [The essence and aim of politics as part of sociology and the basis of the political sciences], 3 vols. (1893), I, 13. Since the state "rescues individuality from annihilation but carries it to sociation," the state is "the only possible societal structure that succeeds in matching individual satisfaction with social necessities."

According to Ratzenhofer—and it is indeed typical of the metaphysical nature of the so-called positivistic concept of science—all sociology is necessarily based upon "the monistic worldview, according to which the law that governs societal life is the same law that the universe is subject to. *Social laws are modalities of the universally valid laws of nature.*"

And Ludwig Gumplowicz writes in his *Geschichte der Staatstheorien,* 2nd impr. (1905), p. 455: "Only with the knowledge that 'politics is the vital expression of the structures of society,' and that these follow its 'social will' like planets follow their lawful movement—only then does politics become a natural law-conformative phenomenon, can it be observed in a similar way to the orbits of celestial bodies, and can its law-conformative behaviors be subsumed under general norms."

[17] See Wilhelm Ostwald, *Energetische Grundlagen der Kulturwissenschaft* [The energetic foundations of the science of culture] (1909), p. 145: "Since law is exclusively a social construct, with the task to abolish an avoidable *waste of energy* in the interaction of its members, *in the same way the reactions against a breach of law, which it requires and carries through, are to be understood exclusively in terms of the same point of view.* To use the customary word *punishment* for this certainly characterizes in a most graphic way the descent of law from the slave relationship, although it does not correspond to the cultural height of the different relationship in which we find ourselves today."

[18] F. Tönnies, *Thomas Hobbes, der Mann und der Denker*, 2nd enl. ed. (1922), pp. 104, 106 (ital. added).

[19] Ludwig Gumplowicz, *Grundrisz der Soziologie* [Outline of sociology], 2nd impr. (1905), p. 300: "Law is a social creation, that is, a form of living together produced by the clash of heterogeneous groups unequal in power."

A similar position is found in the thought of Friedrich von Wieser. In his lecture series *Recht und Macht* [Law and power] (1910), pp. 58–61, he defines law as "the order generated by a community in order to unfold the maximum of its values with a minimum of friction." Or more briefly: "Law is a function of power." Now if Wieser equates power with "values," then it merely means the familiar category shift from the domain of nature to that of values. See also Ignatz Kornfeld, *Soziale Machtverhältnisse* [Social power relationships] (1911), pp. 35ff.

[20] Cf. Emil Kraepelin: "It is altogether true that punishment in its current meaning ceases to be punishment the moment it is turned into a purely protective measure. But precisely in this we observe the greatest achievement of the new views." *Monatschrift für Kriminalpsycholgie und Strafrechtsreform* 3 (1906): 269.

Nevertheless, these naturalists, too, who have thus far been *consistent*, have not avoided antinomies, for that is possible only if they abandon the political import of their system and renounce every intention to influence life through the legal system.

[21] Andreas Thomsen, *Das Deutsche Strafrecht* [German Penal Law] (1907), p. 55, concedes to Karl von Birkmeyer, *Was läst von Liszt vom Strafrecht übrig?* [What is left of penal law in Liszt?] (1906) that the modern school indeed cannot uphold penal law. Thomson exhorts Franz von Liszt and his adherents to let go of the "obsolete system of penal law" and to replace it with a "system of protective law."

[22] Alfred Freiherr von Overbeck, "Die Erscheinungsformen des Verbrechens im Lichte der modernen Strafrechtsschule," [The empirical forms of crime in light of the modern school of penal law], in *Kritische Beiträge zur Strafrechtsreform* [Critical contributions to the reform of penal law] (1909), pp. 2ff. See also Ernst Beling, *Die Vergeltungsidee und Ihre Bedeutung für das Strafrecht* [The idea of retribution and its significance for penal law] (1908).

[23] Cf. Enrico Ferri's study in *Zeitschrift für die gesammte Strafrechtswissenschaft* [Journal for the Combined Discipline of Criminal Law] 41 (1921): 473ff.; Adolf Lenz, *Ein Strafgesetzbuch ohne Schuld und Strafe* [A penal code without guilt or punishment] (1922), p. 14. Furthermore, see the overview of the Italian bill in Professor Zevenbergen's *Leerboek van het Nederlandsche Strafrecht* [Handbook of Dutch criminal law] (1924), 492ff.

It deserves notice that for the sociological school of criminal law, which dominates the Italian bill, compensation for loss caused by a crime entails an eminent part of the protection of society against crime. This corresponds completely with the concepts of the so-called energetic school in sociology. For example, Ostwald, in his *Energetische Grundlagen*, regards such a compensation for loss as the first principle of law in regulating the social use of energy.

Notes to 2.2 The idealist–functionalist type. The Marburg School in neo–Kantian legal theory

[1] On the question regarding the possibility of having knowledge of the divine legal order, see my study, "Calvinisme contra Neo–Kantianisme," *Tijdschrift voor Wijsbegeerte* 1 (1926): 29–75.

[2] According to Cohen continuity as the law of thought is the "conditio sine qua non" of the logic of the origin. See his *Logik der reinen Erkenntnis* (1914), p. 92.

[3] See his *Ethik des reinen Willens*, 4th impr. (1921), pp. 85–94, 104f.

[4] In essence, Stammler's thought is still static, even though for him the legal categories became thought methods. Just observe the path along which he has found his table of categories in his work *Theorie der Rechtswissenschaft* [Theory of the science of law] (1911), pp. 180ff.). Here the functional, dynamic view of categories that we meet in Cohen, Natorp, and Cassirer is nowhere carried through. The legal categories, deduced two by two, maintain their static character in Stammler, just as the four basic elements of his concept of law are static and in no way acquired along the road of functional continuity. For that matter, as we shall discuss below in connection with the problem of form and content,

Stammler got stuck in the same antinomy in which Kelsen and his school became entangled. The only thing Stammler did was to replace the relation between form and content with that of *form* and *matter*. Moreover, he fell prey to still another antinomy, one that cannot but arise when the sovereign boundaries between the jural and the economic are not observed. For Stammler, law is the "logically conditioned" form for economic matters. He wants to assign a relative independence to economic theory yet denies economic matters any independent status; see his work *Wirtschaft und Recht nach der materialistischen Geschichtsauffassung. Eine sozialphilosophische Untersuchung* [Economy and law according to the materialist view of history: A social-philosophical inquiry], 3rd rev. ed. (1914). Notice the hotbed of antinomies and logical contradictions, justifying Max Weber's well–known critique of Stammler.

[5] A more extensive analysis and critique of the views of the normative school of law that was possible in the text is found in my as yet unpublished study of 1921, *Normatieve Rechtsleer. Een kritisch-methodologisch onderzoek* [A Normative Theory of Law: A Study in Critical Methodology]. In this study I have also analyzed Kelsen's transition from a static to a dynamic standpoint. In the Foreword to the second edition of his *Hauptprobleme* (1923) Kelsen himself highlighted the differences between his present and his former standpoint. The definitive transition to the functionalistic-dynamic point of view already took shape in his work *Das Problem der Souveränität und die Theorie des Völkerrechts: Beitrag zu einer reinen Rechtslehre* [The problem of sovereignty and in-

ternal law: Toward a pure law theory] (1920). This transition explains all the specific points of difference, particularly the altered conception of a legal personality, the identification of law and state, abandoning the earlier standpoint that in a static sense all law is contained in statutory law, etc. etc.

⁶ Cassirer's work *Substanzbegriff und Funktionsbegriff* remains instructive for the opposition between the old subsumption logic that is built upon the substance concept, and the modern logic of relations that is rooted in the concept of function.

⁷ See Kelsen, *Allgemeine Staatslehre*, pp. 18–19, 47ff. This is undoubtedly a remnant of the old static Kantian view of two worlds which in the first edition of his work on *Hauptprobleme* served as an unquestioned axiom of his world and life view, a postulate beyond discussion. See also his study "Die Rechtswissenschaft als Norm- oder als Kulturwissenschaft" [The science of law as a normative or cultural discipline], *Schmoller's Yearbook* (1916): 95ff., where Kelsen appeals to Johann Friedrich Herbart (1776–1841). But we have seen how the Marburg School also maintains the law of continuity between ethics and logic. Here the *ought* became *pure will* because it was not accepted as a static given but as something arising from or created by its origin.

More in line with the Marburg School was Fritz Sander in his earlier works. While rejecting the normative character of law, he chose the pure will to function as origin in the process of legal proceedings; cf. his articles: "Das Faktum der Revolution und die Kontinuität der Rechtsordnung" [The *de facto* condition of revolution and the continuity of the legal order]; "Die transcendentale Methode der Rechtsphiloso-phie und der Begriff des Rechtsverfahrens" [The transcen-dental method of legal philosophy and the concept of legal action]; "Alte und neue Staatsrechtslehre" [The old and the new theory of constitutional law]; and "Rechtsdogmatik oder Theorie der Rechtserfahrung" [Systematic jurispru-dence, or the theory of legal experience]—all published in the *Zeitung für öffentliches Recht* 1 (1919/20): 132ff., 468ff., and 2 (1921): 176ff., 525ff. Not that Sander's position is a "pure" element in the sense of the Marburg School, as little as it is in Kelsen's hypothesis of the origin of law. Kelsen, however, is back in line with Cohen when he once again affirms the postulate regarding the independence of the sci-ence of law vis-à-vis the other disciplines and grounds this in the creative "norm–logic."

[8] See Kelsen, *Allgemeine Staatslehre*, p. 54: "*Law as the ob-ject of jural knowledge*—and only under this aspect is it pos-sible to speak of jural law-conformity—is a system of judg-ments, not of imperatives; these judgments, as legal material, may belong to law as it is constituted in jural knowledge. The facts as such may be, among other things, imperatives. The law, as a legal *statute*, is the *legal proposition or legal state-ment*; it is a hypothetical judgment."

In this connection Kelsen also argues that the concept "norm–addressee" cannot mean anything else but that a specific human action forms the content of a legal norm. But since in the "determined state of affairs" also legal facts could be in play—albeit always in connection with human action—the legal norm could just as well "address" events like these. However, the fact that events like these are not allowed to function as "norm addressees" results from the fact that the concept of a "norm addressee" entails law's transcendent purpose or goal, namely the law-conforming actions of human beings. In his earlier works Kelsen also rejected the "norm addressee" as essential element of law. Yet he is uncertain and can't help but lapse into the theory of imperatives. See for example his article "Zur Lehre vom öffentlichen Rechtsgeschäft" [Towards a theory of public legal action], *Archiv des öffentlichen Rechts* 31 (1913): 69, where he acknowledges that a norm can only be binding to those who are normed by it, in other words to those "to whom it is addressed." Despite his rejection of the conception of the "ought-to-be subject" (*Soll-subjekt*) as the addressee of the norm, he repeatedly speaks, in his *Hauptprobleme*, about the fact that "the person for whom the ought-to-be holds [is] the person to whom the ought-to-be is addressed."

The reason for Kelsen's uncertainty must be sought in his static conception of a legal personality as an independent accountable subject vis-à-vis the norm, a conception still found in his earlier works. See also *Hauptprobleme*, p. 434 and, by way of contrast, *Der soziologische und der juristische Staatsbegriff*, pp. 134–135, where this static concept of a person is totally replaced by a dynamic one.

⁹ *Allgemeine Staatslehre*, p. 47.

¹⁰ Kelsen appears to equate goal and content of law, hence runs into the antinomy that the content of law must

be transcendent to law. See *Allgemeine Staatslehre*, p. 40. We shall return to this antinomy below.

[11] *Allgemeine Staatslehre*, pp. 48 ff. Of course, as a result of his functionalization of the concept of a legal subject, Kelsen's concept of imputation is fundamentally altered. When he still adhered to the static point of view, he viewed imputation as attribution to the static legal subject as an "ought-to-be subject."

[12] In connection with personification as fiction, see an older study of Kelsen which he wrote under the influence of Vaihinger's *Philosophie des Als ob* [The Philosophy of As if]. It is entitled "Zur Theorie der juristischen Fiktionen" [Towards a theory of juristic fictions], *Annalen der Philosophie* I (1919): 630 ff.

[13] *Allgemeine Staatslehre*, p. 58. In his *Hauptprobleme* Kelsen already construes a subjective right as a *secondary* form of appearance of the *Rechtssatz*, whose authentic manifestation is the *legal obligation*. The *subjective* right of the [citizen as] subject is then the *Rechtssatz* in its relation to the person, whose claim is made dependent upon some or other action of the will of the state as declared in the *Rechtssatz*. Of course, so long as he adhered to a static concept of law, Kelsen could not conceive a subjective right as a delegation to lower jural levels by a higher level. See *Hauptprobleme*, pp. 556 and 562ff. The entire character of the process of creating law as a social function is banned from the pure theory of law (see his conception of legislation, pp. 410ff.).

[14] *Allgemeine Staatslehre*, pp. 60 ff.

[15] "Eine Bedingung des mit ihm rechtssatzmässig verknüpften Zwangsaktes, der sogenannten Unrechtsfolge." Ibid., p. 52.

[16] Professor Adolf Merkl first developed his theory of the tiered structure of law in his two studies "Das Recht im Lichte seiner Anwendung" [Law in the light of its application], *Deutsche Richterzeitung* 9 (1917), and "Das doppelte Rechtsanlitz" [The double face of law], *Juristische Blätter* 47 (1918), and more broadly in, among other places, his most recent work, *Die Lehre von der Rechtskraft, entwickelt aus dem Rechtsbegriff* [The theory of legal force, developed from the concept of law] (1923), pp. 201ff.

The doctrine of one-level statute law that Kelsen had accepted in his earlier works was essentially nothing but a dogmatic legacy of humanist natural law (cf. the dispute about codification between Savigny and Thibaud). It had already been unmasked by Ernst Rudolf Bierling and Albert Hänel, and also by Oskar Bülow in his important study *Gesetz und Richteramt* [Statute law and the office of judge] (1885). Moreover, Merkl has stated openly that he all he has done is to develop further the lines laid out by these forerunners.

Fritz Sander, in his study *Kelsens Rechtslehre: Kampfschrift wider die normativen Jurisprudenz* [Kelsen's legal theory: A polemic against the Normative School of Jurisprudence] (1923), pp. 28ff., has rightly remarked about Merkl's and Kelsen's view of the tiered structure of law that they have managed to create not a *jural* but only a *logical, natural-law* continuity between the tiers of law and so allowed the legal order itself to remain stuck in the discontinuity of systematic jurisprudence. Sander, by contrast, in his above-mentioned article about the "Theorie des Rechtsverfahrens," attempts to base the continuity of law in *Rechtsverfahren* (legal action) itself, an attempt in which he was bound to run stuck, just like the teachers of the Norm-logic School whom he wanted to refute, because the continuity principle here intended bears a mathematical, natural–scientific character.

[17] Kelsen, *Allgemeine Staatslehre*, pp. 262ff.

[18] Ibid., p. 250.

[19] See the early essay by A. von Verdross, "Zur Konstruktion des Völkerrechts" [Toward the construction of international law], *Zeitschrift für Völkerrechts* 8 (1919): 329–359.

[20] Verdross, "Grundlagen und Grundlegungen des Völkerrechts" [Laying the foundations of international law], *Niemeyer's Zeitschrift für Internationales Recht* 29 (1921): 65ff.

[21] Verdross, *Die Einheit des rechtlichen Weltbildes auf Grundlage des Völkerrechtsverfassung* [The unity of the legal world-picture on the basis of prevailing international law] (1923).

[22] Ibid., p. 134.

[23] Ibid., pp. 135–136.

²⁴ Ibid., p. 124.

²⁵ Ibid., p. 138n.

²⁶ W. Henrich, *Theorie des Staatsgebietes* [The theory of state territory] (Leipzig and Vienna, 1923). See also his article "Zur Theorie der Rechtskraft" [Towards a theory of legal validity], *Archiv des öffentlichen Rechts*, N.T., 7.3 (1924): 329ff.

²⁷ Cohen, in his *Ethik des reinen Willens* [The ethics of pure will] (1921), pp. 273ff., qualifies the "ought to be" not as a constitutive direction of judgment, but merely as a category of modality in the Kantian sense. In opposition to Kelsen he thus positions *Sollen* outside any comparison with natural–scientific causality as a relational category. The "ought to be" is for him no constitutive condition, like a natural law, but rather is on a par with *necessity* as a modal category in a Kantian sense. *Sollen* is "law–conforming *Wollen*" (will or intention) and distinguishes itself from *Sein* in two respects: (i) through its generality, and (ii) through its directedness towards the future. Through both these features *Sollen* distinguishes itself from *Sein* as a *goal principle*. For this reason Cohen cannot see the norm as a judgment, as Kelsen does. To anyone who is at all familiar with Kant's line of reasoning it will be clear that the Kantian modality is not a sovereign, qualitative category and therefore not in the least capable of guaranteeing the sovereignty of the jural sphere. And within the functionalistic "generating methodology" of Cohen the possibility is even smaller that *modality* could ac-

quire this meaning. In Cohen's thought, generality, like the category of time, remains a sovereign creation of continuous thought and therefore it is more difficult for him to escape from the basic antinomy of the humanistic law–idea than it would have been for Kant.

[28] To an even more shocking degree than in Kelsen, the confusion between modality (in our sense) and relation comes to expression in the thought of his pupil Felix Kaufmann. In his work *Logik und Rechtswissenschaft: Grundriss eines Systems der reinen Rechtlehre* [Logic and the Science of Law: Outline of a system of pure law theory] (1922), p. 89, Kaufmann posits that jural imputation is what is typical of a legal norm. Through the specific nature of jural imputation the *Rechtssatz* (legal statement) acquires a strange "double–layered" character. "A subject S is to perform an action A_1; if this is not done, action A_2 ought to take place against that person" (p. 92). In the correlation of these two norms Kaufmann now identifies the specific essence of jural imputation. His argumentation is peculiar: "*Sollen* and norm are correlative concepts; the properties which make a norm into a norm of a specific kind therefore cannot in turn be contained in the *Sollen* itself" (p. 91). As if the relation of imputation, qua *relation*, is not precisely founded in the *Sollen*. The entire difficulty in which the normative school of jurisprudence gets entangled stems from the humanistic law-idea, the continuity postulate of which ruptures sphere sovereignty at every critical point.

²⁹ This is also pointed out by Fritz Sander in his polemical writing against the normative school of jurisprudence; see his above-mentioned attack on *Kelsens Rechtslehre* (1923), p. 96: "First of all it should be remarked that mathematical natural science has more and more replaced the concept of causality with the function concept as a law–conforming correlation of elements. But this meaning is attached to my concept of the function of the real states of affairs of the *Rechtssatz*: The *Rechtssatz* is a law of correlation (imputation) of the elements of real events, which facts are significant for law."

In the last sentence Sander acknowledges in so many words—and this is critical for unmasking the so–called "normative theory of jurisprudence"—that Kelsen's relation of imputation is merely a logical-mathematical relation of co-ordination.

As for Schreier's view, see further down in the main text [in the Remark].

³⁰ Cf. Sander's work, "Die transcendentale Methode der Rechtsphilosophie und der Begriff des Rechtsverfahrens" [The transcendental method of legal philosophy and the concept of legal action], *Zeitschrift für öffentliches Recht* I (1919/20): 968ff., and foremost his writings directed against Kelsen: "Rechtslehre oder Theorie der Rechtserfahrung? Kritische Studie zur Rechtslehre Hans Kelsens" [A theory of law or a theory of legal experience. A critical study of Kelsen's legal theory], *Zeitschrift für öffentliches Recht* 2 (1921): 551–670; cf. Kelsen's reply: "Rechtswissenschaft und Recht" [The science of law and law], *Zeitschrift für öffentliches Recht* II.1/2

(1922). See also Sander's work quoted in the previous note: *Kelsens Rechtslehre* (1923), passim, and his *"Zur Methodik der Rechtswissenschaft"* [On the method of the science of law], which is a polemic against Felix Kaufmann published in *Kantstudien* 28.3/4 (1923): 283ff., and his comprehensive work *Staat und Recht. Prolegomena zu einer Theorie der Rechtserfahrung* [State and law: Introduction to a theory of legal experience] *Wiener Staatswissenschaftlichen Studien*, New Series, Vol. I (1922), and his articles: "Der Begriff der Rechtserfahrung" [The concept of legal experience], *Logos* 11 (1923): 285ff., and "Das Verhältnis von Staat und Recht" [The relation between state and law], *Archiv des öffentlichen Rechts*, New Series, 10.1/2 (1926): 153ff.).

[31] This is done with an appeal to a work by Emil Lask, *Die Lehre vom Urteil* [The theory of judgment] (1912).

[32] See Kelsens *Rechtslehre*, pp. 15ff.). Sander here follows Franz Brentano's theory of the *"temporale Modi des Vorstellens"* [the temporal modes of representation]. See F. Brentano, *Von der Klassifikation der psychischen Phänomene* [On the classification of psychical phenomena] (1911), pp. 131ff., 135.

[33] Sander, *Kelsens Rechtslehre*, pp. 84–85, in a polemic against Cohen: *"The peculiar nature of the regions of consciousness cannot be derived from the* a priori *dogma of some or other "total consciousness," for only a plain and simple analysis of reflection can reveal the essence of the individual regions of consciousness. . . .* Never does 'law' signify a *natural science,*

physics, or *sociology:* for we need only analyse *law* in order to realize at once that it is a *natural science* neither in a noetic sense nor in a noematic sense. Not in a *noetic* sense: for the correlating subject of law is limited to 'organs'; law embraces the noetic axioms of the entitlement of organs, of legal competence, and of jural validity (legal force), as well as the appertaining noetic axioms, which are nowhere to be found in *any* natural science: the jural *procedure* alone is the unity of the noetic legal conditions. Not in a *noematic* sense: for amongst the "points of view" of every neotic legal axiom the "given objects," the "real states of affairs," are presented in a way totally different from the way they occur in natural science. The juridical procedure formulates sovereign conditions of intuition; it is only in correlation with legal procedure that facts are transformed into legal *noema,* into jurally significant facts." Cf. also Edmund Husserl, *Ideen zu einer reinen Phänomenologie und phänomenologische Philosophie* (1913), pp. 108ff., 174ff. Hereafter cited as *Ideen.*

In this entire exposition, Husserl saddles *Rechtsverfahren* ["legal experience"] with a phenomenological meaning that makes a caricature of the action of a judicial organ. Just look at the utter failure of the "phenomenological" analyses of legal judgments (*Ideen,* pp. 101ff.). What is so odd and contradictory about this entire construction is that the actions of organs are at one and the same time serving as "judgments in the sense of transcendental logic" and as constitutive "law–creating judgments," and thereby come to stand in a relation of analogy to the judgments of natural science, while the judgments of the science of law presumably have only a "*reflexive*" character in Husserl's sense, in which sense they would form the analogue of the judgments of a philosophy of nature. Apart from the impossibility to place Sander's *Rechtsverfahren* analogically on the same epistemological *level* as natural science (with Emil Lask, one can at most speak of a pre-scientific formation of concepts within the real formation of law), Sander appears to have lost sight completely of the fact that it is precisely in Husserl's "*reflexion,*" as point of entry of phenomenology, that the problem of "constituting the object" once again surfaces. In his phenomenology Husserl attempted—and was compelled to attempt—to bridge the gap between *act* and *Gegenstand,* demanded by his logical-idealistic standpoint. This was not yet a part of his *Eidetiek* (a theory of pure essences). After all, eidetics finds itself completely enclosed within the essential sphere of *Gegenständlichkeit* and was nothing but a logical operation of identity within the domain of things. But that bridge could only be provided by the idea of *constitutive* formation. And so we also observe that the constitutive element comes to the fore in the *Phänomenologie der Vernunft* (Phenomenology of reason); see the subheading in *Ideen,* p. 309: "*Die vernunfttheoretischen Probleme der regionalen Ontologien. Das Problem der phänomenologischen Konstitution*" (The problems of theoretical reason of regional ontologies. The problem of the phenomenological constitution). In the domain of law and state, too, phenomenological reflexion must address the "problem of constitution" in a phenomenological sense (cf. *Ideen,* p. 318). If Sander had had a better understanding of this state of affairs in Husserl's philosophy, he would immediately have realized that by assigning a purely reflexive character to the science of law he only strengthened the antinomy between his "jural procedure" and his view of the task of the science of law. Sander too remained caught in the antinomy created by the Marburg School between positive law as ordering and the science of law.

More about this antinomy in Sander's system is found in the work of Siegfried Marck, *Substanz- und Funktionsbegriff in der Rechtsphilosophie* [The concepts of substance and function in legal philosophy] (1925), pp. 55ff.

[34] Husserl, *Ideen*, p. 108: "It stands to reason, first of all, that with the *Ausschaltung* [setting aside or suspension] of the natural world, the physical and the psychological objects, too, as well as all the individual objects constituted by the evaluating and practical functions of consciousness, are *ipso facto* set aside … The same naturally applies to realities of the kind to which the state, morality, law, and religion belong. With that, *all the natural sciences and humanities*, with the totality of their factual knowledge, are likewise set aside, as well as those disciplines requiring the natural attitude."

This *Ausschaltung*, this epochè, reveals the fact that in the thought of Husserl, albeit in a sense different from Kant, the enduring tendency of the humanistic knowledge ideal maintains the "sovereign freedom" of consciousness vis-à-vis what is objectively given. When whatever this psychology puts in brackets (the "reality thesis" but also the "value thesis") once again returns in this phenomenology "between quotation marks," and when Husserl maintains the possibility to grasp *adequately* in reflexion what is "given as an object," then he stumbles upon the insoluble antinomy between subject and object which is intrinsic to the whole of idealistic, transcendental philosophy. With great clarity this was unveiled by the father of modern, critical ontology, Nicolai Hartmann (in his *Grundzüge einer Metaphysik der Erkenntnis* [The fundamentals of a metaphysics of knowledge], 2nd enl. ed. (1925) and by Walter Ehrlich in his penetrating work *Kant und Husserl: Kritik der transzendentalen und der phänomenologischen Methode* (1923).

In his phenomenology, too, Husserl remains captive to an *eidetic logicism*, which is based in humanism's metaphysical ideal of knowledge.

The points of view which are only maintained in the "natural attitude of consciousness" are eliminated in Husserl and no longer appear in his phenomenology. His "*Regionen*"—regional categories, regional axioms, and essential laws—are all found on the leveled plane of his logical "*Eidetik*." They are all subsumed under the sphere of the "necessities of thought," the sphere which alone is sovereign in rationalistic humanism.

And it is evidence of the inner weakness of Husserl's phenomenology when it sidesteps the basic question of all critical philosophy, How is it possible to experience a *Gegenstand*? with an appeal to the metaphysical dogma of the thorough-going correlation of *noesis* and *noema* on the one hand and *noema* and *Gegenstand* on the other (see *Ideen*, pp. 265ff.).

This lack of critical reflection, particularly in the case of Sander's thesis that law resides in the sphere of *Sein*, of what *is*, can only prove fatal. The question regarding the possibility of a jural reality next to a causally determined natural reality, a question that cannot be sidestepped by any ideal-istic theory of knowledge, is haughtily set aside by Sander. Truly, not a demonstration of a well–founded and thought-through theory!

The same shortcoming is evident in the swiftness of suc-cessive changes occurring in his basic orientation as well as in the uncritical eclectic way in which he successively manages to accommodate the most diverse philosophical conceptions to his theoretical views of law.

[35] Sander's latest radical change of orientation (his fourth in a short period of time) manifested itself soon after the publication of his polemic of 1923, *Kelsens Rechtslehre*. See his writings: "Othmar Spanns Überwindung der individual-istischen Gesellschaftsauffassung" [Othmar Spann's triumph over the individualistic view of society], *Archiv für Sozial-wissenschaft und Sozialpolitik* 53.1 (1923): 11–80; "Der Ge-genstand der reinen Gesellschaftslehre" [The object of a pure theory of society], *Archiv für Sozialwissenschaft und Sozial-politik* 54.2 (1924): 329–423; "Zum Problem der Soziolo-gie des Rechtes" [On the problem of the sociology of law], *Archiv für Sozialwissenschaft und Sozialpolitik* 55.1 (1925); "Staat und Recht als Probleme der Phänomenologie und Ontologie" [State and law as problems for phenomenolo-gy and ontology], *Zeitschrift für öffentliches Recht* 4 (1924): 788ff.); and finally his study, "Das Verhältnis von Staat und Recht. Eine Grenzauseinandersetzung zwischen allgemeiner Staatslehre, theoretischer Rechtswissenschaft und interpreta-tiver Rechtsdogmatik" [The relation between state and law: An inquiry into the boundaries between the general science

of politics, the theoretical science of law, and interpretive systematic jurisprudence], *Archiv des öffentlichen Rechts*, New Series, 10.1/2 (1926): 153 ff.).

This change in standpoint is interesting insofar as Sander has now radically given up the "creative methodology" of the Marburg School which initially stimulated his entire legal philosophy. The switch shows that Sander has come to understand that it is untenable to combine the functionalistic-logicistic philosophy of the Marburg School with the ontological and phenomenological method. But this at once cancels the "functionalistic" ideal of continuity with its *antinomic postulates*, such as: the unity of state and law, the primacy of the order of international law, the continuity between constitutional law and international law, the elimination of subjective rights, the abolition of the difference between public and private law, etc. etc. Quite a turnabout for someone who failed to understand the deeper unity in all forms of the humanistic law-idea! For those who did observe this deeper unity it is less incomprehensible (the switch illustrates the phenomenon of "polar tensions" in the humanistic law-idea).

[36] See *Das Problem der Souveränität*, pp. 105, 252–253). Cf. also Merkl, "Die Lehre von der Rechtskraft" [The theory of legal force], *Wiener Staatswissenschaftlichen Studien* 15.2 (1923): 209 n. 1), where he chose the following formula as original norm to describe the legal order of the Republic of Austria: "Law is what shall have force according to the decisions of the first German-Austrian Parliament installed after the revolution."

[37] In Kelsen, *Allgemeine Staatslehre*, pp. 239ff., we find an even sharper manifestation of the antinomy of the form-content problem in his formalistic theory of law, namely where he discusses the problem of the genesis of individual states. Here he writes:

> When what is factual becomes the content of a norm it experiences a very peculiar change in meaning: it is denatured, as it were; it turns into its opposite; it becomes normative itself. One should not speak of the "normative force of the factual" but of the metamorphosis of the factual into the normative. Naturally, international law here touches upon the ultimate boundaries of the domain of normative knowledge, upon the ultimate limits of law. It is perhaps still law when it threatens the fundamental opposition of *Sein* and *Sollen,* not while it is concerned to establish just any factual power as a legal force, but merely to allow a specific factual power to have legal force. And it is in this weakness of international law—to capitulate to the facts—that the problem of its jural nature manifests itself more clearly than in its putative lack of coercive power.

Thus, what he introduces here is a "change in meaning" of the factual into a norm-content. But this idea, which for that matter fully floats in thin air in the "Pure Theory of Law," sharply contradicts the formalistic starting point of this entire system, for also in terms of Kelsen's later works the norm-content is denatured to a meta-jural given. Moreover, the skeptical tone in which Kelsen expresses himself in the above-mentioned quotation shows to what extent the problem of the normative content stumped him.

Kelsen's relativistic point of view, which already showed up when he accepted the theoretical equality of the hypothesis regarding the "primacy of constitutional law" and that regarding the "primacy of international law," and which surrendered his entire "empirical methodology of the genesis of law" to a relativistic natural law, is intimately connected with this antinomy inherent in the problem of form and content. After all, no sooner is the content of law identified with the aim of law, than political relativism will lay claim on the science of law itself as a discipline of positive empirical law.

[38] Kelsen, *Hauptprobleme der Staatsrechtslehre*, pp. 42 and 92.

[39] Kelsen, *Allgemeine Staatslehre*, p. 137.

[40] Ibid., p. 54.

[41] Kelsen, *Das Problem der Souveränität*, p. 147 n. 2.

[42] Kelsen, *Der soziologische und der juristische Staatsbegriff*, p. 237.

[43] Kelsen, *Allgemeine Staatslehre*, p. 51.

[44] See Adolf Merkl, *Das Recht im Lichte seiner Anwendung* [Law viewed in the light of its application], p. 11.

[45] Kelsen, *Das Problem der Souveränität*, pp. 252–253.

[46] Kelsen, *Allgemeine Staatslehre*, p. 129.

[47] Merkl, *Die Lehre von der Rechtskraft*, p. 290.

[48] See Kelsen, *"Ueber Staatsunrecht"* [On state injustice], *Grünhutszeitschrift* 40 (1913): 55.

[49] One of the merits of the study of Ernst von Hippel is that it emphatically pointed this out; see his *Untersuchungen zum Problem des fehlerhaften Staatsaktes* [Investigations into the problem of wrongful state acts], enl. ed. (1931).

[50] Merkl, *Die Lehre von der Rechtskraft*, pp. 293ff.

[51] See the fine study of Prof. A. Anema, *De Bronnen van het Privaatrecht* [The sources of private law] (1913), pp. 23 ff.

[52] Merkl, *Die Lehre von der Rechtskraft*, p. 284. Compare what Kelsen writes in his *Allgemeine Staatslehre* (pp. 368 ff.) regarding the connection between democracy as a form of government and the relativistic world and life view which, as we shall see, is in turn founded in the humanistic personality ideal. Nor is it an accident that the relativist Kelsen has committed his heart to democracy! See also his study, *Vom Wesen und Wert der Demokratie* [On the essence and value of democracy] (1920).

Notes to 2.3 The relativistic-personalistic type. The Baden School in neo–Kantian legal theory

[1] The founder of the Baden School, Wilhelm Windelband, explained the relation of this school to the idealism of Fichte and Hegel in his work, *Die Philosophie im Deutschen*

Geistesleben des XIX Jahrhunderts [Philosophy in the intellectual life of Germany during the 19th century] (1909), pp. 119–120. He writes: "We no longer appreciate the transient form of the logical construction of their impressive systems (namely those of idealism), nor the abstract formulas of their metaphysics. But we have gained anew an understanding of the compelling energy with which they, and in particular Hegel, contributed to the entire historical development of the lasting legacy of cultural values and for bringing to consciousness their supra-empirical validity."

[1a] Cf. H. Rickert, *Der Gegenstand der Erkenntnis* [The object of knowledge], pp. 164 ff.; "Zwei Wege der Erkenntnistheorie" [Two directions in epistemology], *Kantstudien* 14 (1909); and "Vom Begriff der Philosophie" [Concerning the concept of philosophy], *Logos* 1 (1910).

[2] Thus Emil Lask, *Rechtsphilosophie*, in *Collected Works* (1923), I, 290.

[3] For Max Weber's standpoint, see esp. his "Die objektivität sozialwissenschaftlicher und sozialpolitischer Erkenntnis" [The objectivity of the knowledge of social science and social politics] *Archiv für Sozialwissenschaft und Sozialpolitik* 19 (1904); republished in his *Gesammelte Aufsätze zur Wissenschaftslehre* (1922), pp. 146–214.

[4] This peculiar relational context postulated for the concept of law also explains the methodological dualism which the Baden School regards as the A B C of jural methodology.

Cf. Lask, *Rechtsphilosophie*, pp. 311–312:

One cannot make headway in the methodology of the science of law without first considering the methodological dualism to which all legal study is subjected, and one is fully justified in calling it the A B C of jural methodology. . . . The twin method of legal science is based upon the fact that on the one hand law can neither be viewed as a *real* cultural factor, as a social life process, nor can it be tested as a complex of *meanings*—to be more precise: of normative meanings—in respect of its dogmatic content. As such, the social theory of law, like all formalistic cultural sciences, isolates an abstraction from concrete social totality, an abstract thing that does not really exist in isolation from its extra-jural environment.

. . . Yet we do not shy away from assigning *reality* also to the objects of the individual formalistic cultural disciplines in which the artificial alienation from the original reality substrate has progressed infinitely further in an epistemological sense. We construct authentic concepts of *cultural* realities, and in this case indeed of abstract *partial* realities, which we set opposite the concrete cultural realities of history.

Lask is fully aware of the methodological difficulty in which he entangles himself; he continues: "At this point, the logic of the formalistic cultural disciplines faces one of its most difficult challenges. It is continually confronted with the question to what extent a cultural scientific approach merely penetrates to the "realities" that are *related to* cultural meanings, and to what extent this approach takes the realm *itself* of pure, isolated meanings" as its final goal. Lask finds the solution in the distinction between the "social theory of law" and the formal science of law: "Law in its social meaning serves as 'real' cultural factor, law in a jural sense as the totality of merely conceived meanings."

[5] In light of this point of view which opposes Stammler, see *inter alia* Julius Binder, *Rechtsbegriff und Rechtsidee* [The concept of law and the idea of law] (1915); Max Weber, *R. Stammlers "Ueberwindung" der materialistischen Geschichtsauffassung"* [R. Stammler's "conquest" of the materialist view of history], *Gesammelte Aufsätze zur Wissenschaftslehre* (1922), pp. 291–395, with an Epilogue at pp. 556–579; Walter Staffel, *"Über Stammlers Lehre vom richtigen Recht"* [On Stammler's theory of right law], *Jahrbücher für die Dogmatik des heutigen römischen und deutschen Privatrechts*, vol. 49, 2nd series, XIII–XIV (1905): 395; Leonhard Cohn, "Das objectiv Richtige" [Objective right], *Kantstudien* 46 (1919); Hermann Kantorowicz, *Die Lehre vom richtigen Recht* [The theory of just law] (1907); and G. A. Wielikowski, *Die Neukantianer in der Rechtsphilosophie* [The Neo–Kantians in Legal Philosophy] (1914), pp. 26ff. In reaction to this last author, see Stammler's rebuttal in *Zeitschrift für Rechtsphilosophie* 2 (1919): 154–170.

[6] Among Radbruch's other works particular mention should be made of the following: *Der Handlungsbegriff* [The Act Concept] (1903), a contribution to the systematic treatment of legal material, a kind of formal, general theory of law, specifically related to the act concept of penal law (still with an uncritical orientation); "Rechtswissenschaft als

Rechtsschöpfung" [The science of law as the creation of law], *Archiv für Sozialwissenschaft*, Neue Folge, IV (1906): 355ff.; *Einführung in die Rechtswissenschaft* [Introduction to the Science of Law], 4th ed. (1919); as well as his studies "*Über den Begriff der Kultur*" [On the concept of culture], *Logos* 11 (1920/21): 200ff.); "Die Problematik der Rechtsidee" [The problem concerning the idea of law], *Jahrbuch für Geisteswissenschaften* 3 (1924): 43ff.; and "Religionsphilosophie der Kultur," *Vorträge der Kantgesellschaft*.

[7] Radbruch, *Grundzüge der Rechtsphilosophie* [Fundamentals of legal philosophy] (1914), p. 29. See also p. 39: "Law is everything that can be made into the object of a statement of justice and also a statement of injustice; Law is that which is supposed to be just law, regardless of whether it truly is just; Law is directed at the goal of Right, without necessarily having reached this aim; Law is the successful or failed attempt to be just law; Law is the ontic structure serving as the substrate and showcase of legal values, the idea of law."

[8] See ibid., pp. 24ff. Typical of this personalistic standpoint is a statement like the one on p. 28: "Politics makes known the means, legal philosophy the contents of a legal ideal—an ideal that cannot be created by knowledge but *only by a will that is born of profound self-reflection from the depth of one's personality*" (ital. added).

Against the reproach that relativism only renews the "resigned cynical question of Pilate, *What is Truth?*—"the decadent blasé attitude that declares all valuations to be equally false"—Radbruch defends relativism with great enthusiasm: Legal philosophy, he writes, does not leave the choice of possible orientations to individual arbitrariness, but to the conscience, to practical reason; . . . " and when the conscience fails to succeed in a methodical way in overcoming the anguish of having to make this choice—when it allows itself to be dissuaded by the multiplicity of individual decisions by other people's conscience, by the multicolored plenitude of moral personalities, by the richness of the moral world in its individual, highly personal morality—then clearly it is a sick conscience and not an erring intellect that has confronted it with the choice."

The strong personalistic imprint of the value relativism of Max Weber—the postulate of the autonomy of the moral personality, which cannot but lead to an unyielding struggle against the importation of value-moments into science—has recently been demonstrated in a most significant way by Robert Wilbrandt in his study, "Max Weber als Erkenntniskritiker der Sozialwissenschaften" [Max Weber as critical epistemologist of the social sciences], *Zeitschrift für die gesammte Staatswissenschaften* 79.4 (1925): 583–675. The author concludes his important analysis with the words: "Thus it has come to pass that *that which Max Weber so carefully tried to avoid* for any individual judgment, is now, through his theory oriented to Windelband and Rickert, inserted into our entire academic discipline: it is a worldview which he mandates once and for all."

[9] Radbruch, *Grundzüge der Rechtsphilosophie*, (1914) p. 40.

[10] Rickert, *System der Philosophie* (1921), p. 308.

[11] See Paul Oppenheim, *Die natürliche Ordnung der Wissenschaften* [The natural order of the sciences] (1926) esp. pp. 40ff. The author is committed to the continuity standpoint of the humanist science ideal, and on the basis of this position he attempts to construct a continuous logical connection between the natural sciences and the humanities. In order to succeed in this, he assigns as poles for every scholarly discipline the ordering principles introduced by the Baden School, namely those of individualizing (i.e., typifying and abstracting) and concretizing. In the gamut of academic disciplines one can then observe a continuous increase of concretizing and individualizing, and even the most abstract sciences are said to possess a certain degree of individualization and concretization.

[12] Radbruch had treated the system of values already earlier, in his study quoted above, "Über den Begriff der Kultur," *Logos* 11 (1920/21): 200ff.

[13] I refer to Emil Lask's very specific theory regarding the relationship between form and content. In his *Die Logik der Philosophie* (1911), Lask points at a deficiency in Kant's theory of categories. Kant remained stuck in the categories of *being*. He did not realize that category itself is in turn *theoretical meaning*, i.e., non-sensory material given in a logical form; this caused the logical form to float in thin air. In order to supplement this deficiency Lask points at the necessity of a "Logic of Philosophy." Regarding the domain of the

sensory (that of *being*), he corrects the views of Rickert and Windelband who resolved the category of being (the specific domain category for the sensory) with the category of validity. Lask shows that the category of being is not a category of validity, for as non-sensory material it belongs to the higher logical form of being valid. Thus, opposed to the specific domain category of the sensory, of *being*, stands its equal, the specific domain category of the non-sensory: of *being valid*.

Lask now explains—and this is what Radbruch is alluding to—that the "pure theoretical form," elevated above all diversity, acquires its specific imprint through its adaptation to the heterological material. In opposition to the logic of origin of the Marburg School, which believed that all categories originate in pure thought, Lask posits the decisive significance of, as he calls it, the "logically naked" and the "logically unaffected" material. The "pure theoretical form," in its adaptation to the heterological material, is burdened by an "irrational element of meaning." This element is already hidden in the categories of being and the category of validity.

The "Logic of Philosophy" teaches that knowing is nothing but using the theoretical form in order to logically embrace irrational material (p. 217). The "differentiation of meaning" of the constitutive categories is found in the material they refer to, and not in logical thought itself.

Here Lask takes an important step in the direction of an irrational metaphysics. See also his work *Die Lehre vom Urteil* [The theory of judgment], where he speaks of "truth an sich."

[14] Radbruch, *Grundzüge der Rechtsphilosophie,* pp. 40ff.

[15] Ibid., pp. 50ff.

[16] Leon Petrazycki, *Über die Motive des Handelns und über das Wesen der Moral und des Rechts* [On the motives of action and the essence of morality and law], trans. from the Russian by P. Balson (1907). The research by this author has a psychologistic orientation.

[17] According to Kelsen a legal order is possible without any subjective right!

[18] Radbruch, *Grundzüge der Rechtsphilosophie,* pp. 54–58.

[19] *Sic venia verbo*: excuse the word (pardon my French).

[20] See Krabbe, *De moderne Staatsidee* (1915), pp. 50ff.). Krabbe regards the "unity of the legal norm" as the highest jural value, because the purpose of society can be achieved through it alone. People's sense of justice, too, assigns the highest value to this unity, even as it abandons, if need be, a content they might otherwise prefer. This road, then, justifies the majority principle. In the case of a qualitative equality of legal sense [i.e., when people have different feelings about what is just] the norms desired by a *majority* will be of higher value.

This strange construction, intended to resolve a basic antinomy by psychologistic means, was universally dismissed, and rightly so.

[21] Radbruch, *Grundzüge der rechtsphilosophie,* pp. 159–160.

[22] Ibid., p. 179.

[23] Cf. Radbruch's views, ibid., pp. 184ff.

Notes to 2.4 Trans-personalist and objectivist-idealist types in legal philosophy

[1] Erich Kaufmann made a similar transition to objective idealism; see both his *Das Wesen des Völkerrechts und die Clausula rebus sic stantibus* [The essence of international law and *clausula rebus sic stantibus*] (1911), and his *Kritik der neukantischen Rechtsphilosophie* [A critique of neo–Kantian legal philosophy] (1921). See also his dissertation: *Studien zur Staatslehre des monarchischen Prinzips* [Studies in the political theory of the monarchical principle] (1906). Like Binder, Kaufmann proceeds from the Baden School; but through a study of Hegel and Fichte (in his later period) he became an adherent of trans-personalist philosophy. In his *Rechtsphilosophie* Binder therefore acknowledges Kaufmann as a partner.

[2] In his *Rechtsbegriff und Rechtsidee* [The concept of law and the idea of law] (1915), as well as in his oration of 1912, *Rechtsnorm und Rechtspflicht* [Legal norm and legal obligation], Binder still fully supported the neo–Kantian standpoint of the Baden School. See in connection with his change of view: *Philosophie des Rechts* (1925), pp. 102ff.

³ Julius Binder, *Philosophie des Rechts*, p. 221. See also his *Rechtsbegriff und Rechtsidee* as well as his discussion of Münch in "Kultur und Recht," *Vierteljahrschrift für Gesetzgebung und Rechtswissenschaft*, New Ser., 27 (1922): 227ff.

⁴ See also Binder, "Beiträge zur Philosophie des deutschen Idealismus" [Contribution to the philosophy of German idealism], *Kantheft* 1924, pp. 27ff.

⁵ Binder, *Philosophie des Rechts*, p. 231.

⁶ Ibid., pp. 108f.

⁷ Ibid., pp. 113ff.

⁸ Ibid., p. 672: "The idealism defended and elaborated here differs from positivism. Positivism still dominates all of the subdisciplines, including criminal law. It is based upon the primacy of theoretical reason, which leads to an annihilation of freedom. Far from clarifying this state of affairs and thus providing a foundation for it, positivism rather highlights the untenability of its own position and thus confirms the necessity of the primacy of freedom. Of course, since freedom exists next to and above the necessity of nature, it cannot be properly understood by the critical approach, but only in terms of an idealist position. What must be done is precisely to comprehend the world of necessity, nature with its coercion, as a free act of the spirit, for the sake of being able to comprehend freedom next to necessity."

[9] Ibid., pp. 791ff. Here Binder makes an appeal to the value theory of Rickert found in vol. I of Rickert's *System der Philosophie.* However, Rickert's value theory deviates substantially from that of Binder. Rickert's standpoint, also found in the thinking of Radbruch, is that philosophy must leave it to the conscience of the moral individual to choose a world and life view, and with that a supreme value that best suits their personal extra- or supra-scientific identity (ibid., p. 407). Nevertheless, philosophy, being a comprehensive worldview, does have the task to set up a formal system of values, albeit an open one.

To this end, philosophy must assume a historical orientation and abstract from the historical cultural objects those values that are attached to the historical reality. With the aid of formal principles, which the general foundational role of philosophy reveals as the precondition for every meaningful life, the values found in this way must then be grouped and placed in a formal system. Each value then is matched on the one hand by cultural goods and on the other by the "behavior of subjects." The choice of a supreme value determines the type of world and life view. The cultural goods and the subjective actions are alternatives: the goods are either non-social entities or social persons. The subjective actions corresponding to this alternative are either *monistic contemplation* or *pluralistic activity.* Furthermore, from the point of view of the completion of time (*"Vollendung"*) these values ought to be grouped into levels (*"Stufen"*; see ibid., pp. 348ff.).

This whole train of thought is not found in the thought of Binder. On the contrary, he rejects every system of values.

[10] Binder, *Philosophie des Rechts*, p. 800: "A restriction is necessary only insofar as it is natural that for philosophy, being an academic discipline, the constitutive basic value must remain the value of *truth* or *knowledge*, under which all the other values are to be subsumed the moment it concerns value-filled reality, to which of course belongs as well the world of the special sciences, including the natural sciences."

[11] Ibid., p. 797: "Therefore in practice one value does allow itself to be played off against another. It is possible that one and the same action falls under different value domains; i.e., that the assessment is accessible according to diverse normative domains. And then it is very well possible that the affirmation, the justification of one evaluative perspective could be connected to rejection from the point of view of another value. This applies foremost to works of literature and the fine arts, etc."

[12] Ibid., p. 265. See also *Rechtsbegriff und Rechtsidee* (1915) and Binder's study, "Die Struktur des Rechtsbegriffs" (The structure of the concept of law), in *Festschrift für Paul Hensel* (1923), pp. 92ff.

[13] Binder, *Philosophie des Rechts*, p. 263.

[14] Ibid., p. 265.

[15] Ibid., p. 237.

[16] Ibid., p. 241.

[17] Ibid., p. 354. Cf. also Binder's study, *Recht und Macht als Grundlagen der Staatswirksamkeit* [Law and Power as the bases of state activity] (1921) pp. 17ff. and n. 91.

[18] Binder, *Philosophie des Rechts*, p. 335. He defended the same position already in his oration of 1912 entitled *Rechtsnorm und Rechtspflicht*, which earned him the reproach of jural "nihilism" from Leonard Nelson in his well-known work *Die Rechtswissenschaft ohne Recht* [The science of law without law] (1917), pp. 204f.

In the 1912 oration Binder defended the position that the legal norm is only a hypothetical judgment in a logical sense and in no way addresses the people, the subjects, but must be conceived as a coercive ordinance in case of a default in contract obligations. For this reason, argued Binder, the concepts of default and guilt, and contract as a legal obligation, must be dropped and replaced by the concept "*Haftung*," i.e., as a responsibility or liability (pp. 14f.). Thus he is quite consistent when he states: "One cannot speak of norms of law." See also his *Rechtsbegriff und Rechtsidee*, 189 n. 29, and *Recht und Macht*, pp. 17ff. and n. 91.

[19] Ibid., p. 334.

[20] Ibid., p. 335: "Of course Hegel is mistaken when he denies the merely legal character of the state in his view that the state is purely the realization of morality. Stahl already took exception to this view. Statehood does not mean the

conquest of *abstract* law by means of coercion directed against individual self-will. For the state itself is situated within this abstract law as an institution of law and coercion." See also § 29 of this work [Hegel's *Philosophie des Rechts*].

[21] Ibid., p. 495.

[22] Ibid., p. 435. Cf. also Hegel's formulation in *Philosophie des Rechts,* § 36, of what he regards as "law's imperative," as the essential meaning of a legal order: "Be a person and show respect for the other as person."

[23] Ibid., p. 427.

[24] Ibid., p. 538: "According to this transpersonal understanding of the state, sovereignty attaches neither to the government nor to the people. Thus, one can only speak of *state sovereignty*, and the relationship between state authority and those governed by it cannot be viewed as a relationship of subject and object, or as a means to an end. Individual persons, therefore, do not participate in sovereignty, for they are rather parts of the whole. Just like the government, individuals in their particular individuality and tasks share in the interests, eventualities, and will of the state. In essence, the will of the state is the will of the individual. Consequently, *fundamental rights and human rights cannot play a role in the state*, paramount though they may be in all liberal constitutions." (ital. added)

[25] Ibid., pp. 570, 582.

[26] Ibid., p. 584.

[27] Ibid., pp. 920–921.

Notes to Chapter 3
The Antithesis Between the Christian and the Humanist Law-idea

[1] For the historical basis of the following brief overview of the development of the Christian law-idea I must refer to my series of articles entitled "In den strijd om een Christelijke staatkunde. Proeve eener fundeering der Calvinistische levens- en wereldbeschouwing in hare wetsidee," *Anti–Revolutionaire Staatkunde* (monthly), vols. 1 and 2 (1924/25 and 1925-26), concluded in *Anti-Revolutionaire Staatkunde* (quarterly), vol. 1 (1927). [Eng. trans., *The Struggle for a Christian Politics: An Essay in Grounding the Calvinistic Worldview in Its Law-Idea*, Series B, Vol. 5 in *The Collected Works of Herman Dooyeweerd* (2008).]

See also my *Calvinisme en Natuurrecht* [Calvinism and natural law] (1924), pp. 3ff. [Eng. trans., "Calvinism and Natural Law." In *Essays in Legal, Social, and Political Philosophy*, ed. by Alan M. Cameron et al. *The Collected Works of Herman Dooyeweerd*, Series B, Vol. 2 (1996), pp. 3–38.]

² Through a seemingly insignificant change of a single letter: namely, replacing the metaphysical concept of essence (*entelecheia* – in its Aristotelian sense) by the neutral concept *endelecheia* (about the authenticity of which in Aristotle's works Melanchtons carried on a fierce polemic), Melanchton hollowed out the entire metaphysical foundation of Aristotle's philosophy. In line with nominalism, Melanchton denied the reality of universals, with the result that the Aristotelian theory of substantial forms was stripped of all creative power.

Melanchton had no other option, because Aristotelian metaphysics clashed too seriously with the reformational doctrine of nature and foremost with the sovereignty of the divine will. Actually, in order to accomplish a reconciliation between nature and grace, Melanchton drew less from Aristotle and more from Galenus and nominalistic Stoicism (Cicero).

It is the great merit of Heinrich Maier that he subjected Melanchton's system to a penetrating analysis in light of its law-idea; cf. his important work, *An der Grenze der Philosophie: Melanchton, Lavater, David Friedrich Strauss* (1909), pp. 123ff.). This is all the more significant since Humanism in general showed very little interest in the law-idea. Maier is correct in appreciating the law-idea as "the inner bond that unites the different parts [in Melanchton's thought) into a system" (ibid., p. 123).

³ In this regard I can accept to a certain degree, at least in respect of Melanchton's philosophical ideas, what Dilthey did in his *Weltanschauung und Analyse des Menschen seit Renaissance und Reformation* [Worldview and analysis of man

since Renaissance and Reformation], *Gesammelte Schriften*, vol. II (1923), pp. 164ff. Dilthey treats Melanchton's philosophical views as a link in the development of the natural system of a world and life view. Apart from that, this study suffers from humanism's common error of leveling the absolute antithetical difference between the world and life view of Christianity and that of humanism to something merely relative.

[4] See the brilliant oration *Souvereiniteit in eigen kring* [Sphere sovereignty] with which Kuyper opened the Free University in Amsterdam on October 20, 1880. In this oration an inimitable sketch is given of the thoroughgoing antithesis between the Christian and the Humanistic world and life view in their significance for scholarship. As well, see in particular Kuyper's Stone lectures on Calvinism (1898).

[5] In my study "Calvinisme contra Neo–Kantianisme" [Calvinism versus neo-Kantianism], *Tijdschrift voor Wijsbegeerte rom* (1926): 29–74, I took issue solely with this conception of analogy.

In this connection, see also my summary analysis of the philosophical difference between the Thomist and the Calvinist law-idea. The theory of substantial forms can never be revived by Calvinism, for it is attached to a view of nature that directly contradicts the reformational view, and it served as the basis for the Catholic *mediation* theory between nature and grace. It is also utterly in conflict with the Calvinist understanding of the law as boundary.

[6] Thus, Kant, in his *Prolegomena*, par. 58, defines analogy as a "perfect similarity of relations between the members of two quite dissimilar pairs of things." This gives modern relational logic a free hand for applying its continuity ideal over the entire range of human experience. See also Cohen, *Logik der reinen Erkenntnis*, pp. 359f.

[7] The conception of sphere sovereignty will not hamper scientific thinking in any field of research. Within its own divine boundaries, sphere sovereignty will rather stimulate scientific thinking, enabling it to grasp to the ultimate degree the *Gegenstand* within the logos.

This view also does not know anything of a "closed system" of sovereign spheres; on the contrary, it remains open to the discovery of new spheres. But sphere sovereignty will always remain a barrier to the metaphysical science ideal with its belief in the omnipotence of the scientific method as used in the natural sciences. Sphere sovereignty, based on the one hand in the limiting character of the law and on the other in the organic-cosmological idea of unity, is the critical point of departure *kat! exochen* (par excellence), and it is particularly more critical than Kant's critique of reason.

An instructive example is provided by psychology. For some time, people believed that the *Weber-Fechner Law* bridged the gap between the physical and the psychical in a logical way and that psychological phenomena, too, could be comprehended by means of the quantitative mathematical method. But Act Psychology has shown that this mathematical law remains stuck in the boundary region, in the substrate of the psychical sphere, without being able to approximate the psychical *Gegenstand* as such. On this, see Binswanger, *Einführung in die Probleme der Allgemeinen Psychologie,* [Introduction to the problems of general psychology] (1922), pp. 82ff.

⁸ At bottom, one finds the same view regarding the knowing subject in Kuyper, in his *Encyclopaedie der Heilige Godgeleerdheid* [Encyclopedia of sacred theology], vol. II, 2nd rev. ed. (1909), pp. 18ff. This work often reveals intuitively the deepest philosophical insights.

More recently, Nicolai Hartmann, in his work cited earlier, *Grundzüge einer Metaphysik der Erkenntnis* [Fundamentals of the metaphysics of knowledge], 2ⁿᵈ impr. (1925), pp. 307ff., attempted, from a critical ontological point of view, to solve the antinomic subject–object problem of humanism's approach by "embedding" both in the ontological sphere of being: "The epistemological approach, following *ratio cognoscendi*, shows how beings as objects of knowledge become partially known; the ontological approach, following *ratio essendi*, shows how knowledge, together with its objects, is determined by the world of being that underlies and binds them" (p. 307). This, however, is still far from an approximation by Hartmann of the Calvinistic line of thought. In the final analysis, humanism cannot cut its lifestring. Nonetheless the work of Hartmann continues to intrigue.

Notes to Chapter 4
The Significance of the Calvinist Law-idea for Science and Philosophy of Law

[1] *General Editor:* the term *geldingstijd* (a time-bound period of validity) can be attached, for example, to an eviction order, an exemption order, or a statute of limitation. This brief example seems to imply that at this time Dooyeweerd still thought of time as a separate law-sphere, an idea which he abandoned soon afterward.

[1a] In our train of thought, the term "substrate" (*hypokeimenon*) ought to be freed from the Aristotelian idea of substance. We employ the term *sub*-strate in the neutral cosmological sense of *underlying* support, embracing both the sensory and supersensory realities. In particular, this cosmological substrate naturally cannot enter into a judicial judgment. Yet the meaning of the substrates is so fundamental for law that law would disappear into nothingness if these substrates did not serve law as a foundation in a cosmological sense. For in that case the analogies, too, would dissolve, and along with it the jural modality itself. That is how stringently the organic law-idea must be carried through in each of the sovereign spheres.

[2] I say this in opposition to the Marburg School, in particular against Cohen's conception of the mathematical-logical analogy in the concepts *individual* (unity), *society* (multiplicity), and *state* (totality); see Cohen, *Logik der reinen*

Erkenntnis, pp. 142, 202.

[3] This is the correct core in Gierke's concept of the "inclusive person" (*Gesammtperson*) and the "collective will" (*Gesammtwille*), although even this outstanding jurist repeatedly violates sphere sovereignty as he develops his theory. On the other hand, E. I. Bekker's well-known *personification theory* illustrates what humanistic theory of law must come to when it negates the substrates of the jural sphere and, in its penchant for abstraction, attempts to comprehend law as a totally isolated sphere. For Bekker, even "things," in particular *order papers* and *bearer papers*, are turned into legal subjects, which is only possible of course after denaturing the whole concept of legal person; see his article "Die Geldpapiere" [financial documents], *Jahrbuch des gemeinen Deutschen Rechts* 1 (1857): 266ff.

[4] This also needs to be said about the theory of authority as taught by Lohman. [Professor Alexander de Savornin Lohman joined the law faculty of the Free University in 1884 with an inaugural oration, afterwards published under the title *Over het hoogste gezag* [On the supreme authority] (1884).]

[5] I tried to apply this line of thought for the first time in a concrete way in my article about "co−determination in industry," *Antirevolutionaire Staatkunde* 2 (1926): 1–21. See also my article on this topic, "De band met het beginsel" [The bond with our principle], in the bimonthly *Nederland en Oranje* 7 (1926): 2–18, 33–40.

[6] See my tract of 1924, cited above, *Calvinisme en Natuurrecht*, pp. 18ff. [Eng. trans., pp. 3–38].

[7] This is what Rudolf Stammler does. In his neo–Kantian idea of law as the "community of free willing people," he breaks up political natural law in the interest of ethics. No wonder that he appreciates the command of the Christian doctrine "Love your brother" first of all as a rule of objectively correct law ("richtiges Recht") insofar as this commandment norms the mutual relations between people as neighbors; cf. his *Lehrbuch der Rechtsphilosophie* [Handbook of legal philosophy] (1922), pp. 203–204, n. 6.

Nor is it surprising that in his work *Die Lehre von dem richtigen Rechte* [The theory of correct law] (1902), p. 59, Stammler asked in all seriousness why a legal order does not also regulate friendship relations, for example in respect of gifts and succession law.

[8] M. E. Mayer, *Rechtsphilosophie* [Philosophy of law] (1922), p. 94: "For this reason the cultural norms are the values that set the standard for the creation and application of legal norms. Thus, every legal ideal conforms to a cultural ideal and consequently law has to look for its justification in cultural criticism. It would be an understatement to say that law serves culture; *as critical power it also governs it*" (ital. added).

As he continues his exposition, Mayer traces his postulate—that the formation of law be critically oriented to culture—back to the idea of humanity! With humanistic exuberance this idea of *Humanität* is then depicted as "standing sublime in its elevation *above* praxis in its godlike nature (a nature that Herder was happy to assign to it), and sending its cultural endeavors like apostles to every nation . . . teaching them to observe all things whatsoever I have commanded you"!

Notes to the Acknowledgments

[1] [As is customary in Dutch universities, an inaugural oration concludes with some personal addresses.]

[2] [After a short career in the civil service, Dooyeweerd from 1922 to 1926 served as Deputy Director (under party leader H. Colijn) of the *Dr. Abraham Kuyperstichting*, the thinktank and clearing house of the Anti-Revolutionary Party.]

[3] [In the decade following the death of Abraham Kuyper, the Reformed (*gereformeerde*) people of the Netherlands faced doctrinal disputes in the church and uncertainty about the direction of their political party.]

[4] [Willem Zevenbergen (1884–1925), professor of law, died unexpectedly at the age of 41 as the result of an illness. He taught criminal law and philosophy of law.]

[5] [*In magnis et voluisse sat est:* In great endeavors it is enough to have been willing.]

⁶ [Herman Dooyeweerd enrolled at the Free University in 1912 and earned the degree of Doctor of Law in 1917.]

⁷ [The subjects assigned to Dooyeweerd were the theory and philosophy of law and the history of Dutch law.]

⁸ [Dooyeweerd accepted his appointment at the Free University more or less on condition that Dirk Vollenhoven, his brother-in-law and intellectual comrade, would be appointed at the same time as professor of systematic philosophy. In the years that they lived together in The Hague, the two men collaborated in developing the rudiments of a reformational philosophy. In a letter to H. Colijn, director of the Kuyper Institute as well as a member of the university's Board of Directors, Dooyeweerd confided that "the main thing for me [in considering acceptance of the appointment] was that the chair for philosophy be filled by the only man who at this time is able to work out the Calvinist principles for this important terrain. That man is my brother-in-law Dr. Vollenhoven. You will recall, perhaps, that he and I have worked together from the beginning and are of one mind. The evenings and nights in which we talked together and inspired each other are unforgettable to me." Colijn saw the importance of this request and persuaded the university's Board of Curators to accede to it. See Marcel E. Verburg, *Herman Dooyeweerd: The Life and Work of a Christian Philosopher* (Grand Rapids, MI: Paideia Press, 2015), p. 92n. See also Anthony Tol, *Philosophy in the Making: D. H. Th. Vollenhoven and the Emergence of Reformed Philosophy* (diss., Vrije Universiteit, 2010).]

[9] Paul Fabius taught philosophy of law, constitutional law, and canon law.

[10] What you have inherited from your fathers,
make that yours, so that you will possess it!
—Goethe, *Faust*, lines 568f.

BIBLIOGRAPHY

Althusius, Johannes. *Politica methodice digesta atque exemplis sacris et profanis illustrate.* Groningen, 1610.

Anema, A. *De Bronnen van het privaatrecht* [The sources of private law]. Utrecht: Ruys, 1913.

Barnich, Georges. *Essai de politique positive basée sur l'énergétique sociale de Solvay* [Essay in positive politics on the basis of Solvay's social energetics]. Brussels: Lebègue, 1919.

Barth, Paul. *Die Philosophie der Geschichte als Soziologie* [Philosophy of History as Sociology]. Rev. ed. Leipzig: Reisland, 1922.

Bartsch, Helmut. "Die Zukunft der Rechtswissenschaft" [The Future of the Science of Law]. *Archiv für Rechts- und Wirtschaftsphilosophie* 6 *(*1912/13): 127ff.

Bekker, E. I. "Die Geldpapiere" [Financial documents]. *Jahrbuch des gemeinen Deutschen Rechts* 1 (1857): 266ff.

Beling, Ernst. *Die Vergeltungsidee und Ihre Bedeutung für das Strafrecht* [The idea of retribution and its significance for penal law]. Leipzig: Engelmann, 1908.

Binder, Julius. "Beiträge zur Philosophie des deutschen Idealismus" [Contribution to the philosophy of German idealism]. *Kantstudien* 1 (1924).

―――. "Kultur und Recht." *Vierteljahrschrift für Gesetzgebung und RechtsWissenschaft.* N. F., 27 (1922): 227ff.

―――. *Philosophie des Rechts.* Berlin: Stilke, 1925.

―――. *Recht und Macht als Grundlagen der Staatswirk-*

samkeit [Law and power as the bases of state activity]. Erfurt: Keyser, 1921.

———. *Rechtsbegriff und Rechtsidee* [The concept of law and the idea of law]. Leipzig: Deichertsch, 1915.

———. *Rechtsnorm und Rechtspflicht* [Legal norm and legal obligation]. Leipzig: Deicherts, 1912.

———. "Die Struktur des Rechtsbegriffs" [The structure of the concept of law]. Pp. 92ff. in *Festschrift für Paul Hensel.* Greiz im Vogtland: Ohag, 1923.

———. "Der Wissenschaftscharakter der Rechtswissenschaft" [The scientific nature of the science of law]. *Kant studien* 25.4 (1921).

Birkmeyer, Karl von. *Was läst* von Liszt *vom Strafrecht übrig?* [What is left of penal law in Liszt?]. Munich: Beck, 1906.

Bohatec, Josef. "Calvins Vorsehungslehre" [Calvin's doctrine of providence]. Pp. 339ff. in *Calvinstudien: Festschrift zum 400. Geburtstage Johann Calvins.* Leipzig: R. Haupt, 1909.

———. *Calvins Vorsehungslehre.* Halle, 1909.

———. "De organische idee in de gedachtenwereld van Calvijn" [The organic idea in the intellectual make-up of Calvin]. N.pl. N.d.

Bozi, Alfred. *Einführung in das Lebendes Recht* [Introduction to living law]. Hannover: Helwing, 1915.

Brentano, Franz. *Von der Klassifikation der psychischen Phänomene* [On the classification of psychical phenomena].

Leipzig, 1911.

Bülow, Oskar. *Gesetz und Richteramt* [Law and the office of judge]. Leipzig: Duncker & Humblot, 1885.

Calvin, John. Sermons on 1 Sam. 8 and 10. *Corpus Reformatorum* 57: 554–555, 536–637.

Cantor, Georg. Article in *Mathematische Annalen* 46 (1915).

Cassirer, Ernst. *Das Erkenntnisproblem in die Philosophie und Wissenschaft der neueren Zeit.* Berlin: B. Casserer, 1922.

———. *Substanzbegriff und Funktionsbegriff* [Substance Concept and Function Concept] Berlin: B. Cassirer, 1910.

Cohen, Hermann. *Ethik des reinen Willens* [The ethics of pure will]. Berlin: B. Cassirer, 1921.

———. *Logik der reinen Erkenntnis* [the logic of pure knowledge]. 2nd ed. Berlin: B. Cassirer, 1914.

Cohn, Leonhard. "Das objectiv Richtige" [Objective right]. *Kantstudien* 46 (1919).

Dilthey, Wilhelm. *Weltanschauung und Analyse des Menschen seit Renaissance und Reformation* [Worldview and analysis of man since Renaissance and Reformation]. *Gesammelte Schriften*, vol. II (1923).

———. "Das Wesen der Philosophie" [The essence of philosophy]. In Paul Hinneberg, ed. *Die Kultur der Gegenwart.* Berlin: Teubner, 1905.

Dooyeweerd, Herman. "De band met het beginsel. Inzake het vraagstuk der medezeggenschap" [The bond with our principle. On co-determination in industry]. *Nederland en Oranje* 7.1/2 (April/Mei, 1926): 2–18; 7.3 (June, 1926): 33–40.

———. "Calvinisme contra Neo–Kantianisme." *Tijdschrift voor Wijsbegeerte* 1 (1926): 29–75.

———. *Calvinisme en natuurrecht.* Amersfoort: Van Wijngen, 1925 [Eng. trans., "Calvinism and Natural Law." Pp. 3–70 in *Essays in Legal, Social, and Political Philosophy*, ed. by Alan M. Cameron et al. *The Collected Works of Herman Dooyeweerd*, Series B, Vol. 2. Lewiston, NY: Edwin Mellen Press, 1997.

———. *The Collected Works of Herman Dooyeweerd.* D. F. M. Strauss, general editor. Grand Rapids, MI: Paideai Press, 1994– .

———. *Normatieve Rechtsleer. Een kritisch-methodologisch onderzoek* [A normative theory of law: A study in critical methodology]. Unpub. ms. 1921.

———. *The Struggle for a Christian Politics: An Essay in Grounding the Calvinistic Worldview in Its Law-Idea*, Series B, Vol. 5 in *The Collected Works of Herman Dooyeweerd.* Lewiston, NY: Edwin Mellen Press, 2008.

———. "Tweeërlei kritiek. Om de principieele zijde van het vraagstuk der medezeggenschap." [Twofold criticism. Co-determination in industry and our principle]. *Antirevolutionaire Staatkunde* 2 (1926): 1–21.

Durkheim, Emil. *Les formes élementaires de la vie religieuse – le systeme totémique en Australie* [The elementary forms of the religious life: Totemism in Australia]. Paris: Alcan, 1912.

Ehrlich, Eugen. "Die Erforschung des lebenden Rechts [Studying living law]." *Schmollers Jahrbuch* (1911).

———. *Grundlegung der Soziologie des Rechts* [Grounding the sociology of law]. Berlin, 1913.

———. "Ein Institut für lebendes Recht" [An Institute for living law]. *Verhandlungen* des 31. Deutschen Juristen Tages, vol. II.

———. *Die juristische Logik*. 3rd ed. Tübingen: Mohr, 1925.

———. *Kant und Husserl: Kritik der transzendentalen und der phänomenologischen Methode*. Halle an der Saale: Niemeyer, 1923.

Fabius, D. P. D. *Het wezen van het Calvinisme* [The essence of Calvinism]. Kampen: Kok, 1919. Nr. 2.1 in the series *Schild en Pijl*.

Ferri, Enrico. Article in *Zeitschrift für die gesammte Straf rechtswissenschaft* [Journal for the combined discipline of criminal law] 41 (1921): 473ff.

Fichte, J. G. *Grundzügen des gegenwärtigen Zeitalters* [Fundamentals of the contemporary age]. 1806.

———. *Reden an die Deutsche Nation* [Address to the German Nation]. 1807–08.

Görland, Albert. "Der Gottesbegriff bei Leibniz" [The concept of God in Leibniz]. *Philosophischen Arbeiten*, ed. by H. Cohen and P. Natorp. I.3 (Giessen: Töpelmann, 1907).

Groen van Prinsterer, G. *Ter nagedachtenis van Stahl*. Amsterdam: Höveker, 1862. [Eng. trans., *In Memoriam Frie-*

drich Julius Stahl, trans. and ed. by Ruben Alvarado. Aalten, Neth.: Pantocrator Press, 2022.]

Gumplowicz, Ludwig. *Geschichte der Staatstheorien* [History of political theories]. 2nd ed. Innsbruck: Wagner, 1905.

———. *Grundrisz der Soziologie* [Outline of sociology]. 2nd ed. Vienna: Manz, 1905.

Hartmann, Nicolai. *Grundzüge einer Metaphysik der Erkenntnis* [The fundamentals of a metaphysics of knowledge]. 2nd enl. ed. Berlin: De Gruyter, 1925.

Hegel, G. W. F. *Encyclopaedie.* Georg Lasson, ed. Leipzig: Meiner, 1923.

———. *Philosophie des Rechts.* 1821.

Heller, Hermann. *Hegel und der nationale Machtstaatsgedanke im Deutschland* [Hegel and the national power state in Germany]. Berlin: Teubner, 1921.

Henrich, W. *Theorie des Staatsgebietes* [The theory of state territory]. Vienna: Holder-Pichler-Tempsky, 1922.

———. "Zur Theorie der Rechtskraft" [Towards a theory of legal force]. *Archiv des öffentlichen Rechts,* Neue Ffolge, 7.3 (1924): 329ff.

Herder, J. G. *Ideen zu einer Philosophie der Geschichte der Menschheit* [Outlines of a philosophy of the history of mankind]. 4 vols. Leipzig, 1784–91.

Hippel, Ernst von. *Untersuchungen zum Problem des fehlerhaften Staatsaktes* [Investigations into the problem of wrongful state acts]. Enl. ed. Berlin: Springer, 1931.

Hobbes, Thomas. *Corpore politico, or Elements of the law, moral & politic.* London, 1650.

Husserl, Edmund. *Ideen zu einer reinen Phänomenologie* [Ideas for a pure phenomenology]. Halle an der Saale: Niemeyer, 1913.

Husserl, Gerhart. *Rechtskraft und Rechtsgeltung* [Legal force and legal validity]. Berlin: Springer, 1925.

Kant, Immanuel. *Kritik der praktischen Vernunft.* Groszherzog Wilhelm Ernst, ed. Leipzig, 1922.

———. *Kritik der reinen Vernunft.* Groszherzog Wilhelm Ernst, ed. Leipzig, 1922.

———. *Kritik der Urteilskraft.* Groszherzog Wilhelm Ernst, ed. Leipzig, 1922.

Kantorowicz, Hermann. *Die Lehre vom richtigen Recht* [The theory of just law]. Berlin and Leipzig: Rothschild, 1907.

———. *Rechtswissenschaft und Soziologie* [Legal Science and Sociology]. Tübingen: Mohr, 1911.

Kaufmann, Erich. *Logik und Rechtswissenschaft: Grundriss eines Systems der reinen Rechtlehre* [Logic and the science of law: Outline of a system of pure law theory]. Tübingen: Mohr, 1922.

———. *Die Kriterien des Rechts* [The criteria of law]. Tübingen: Mohr, 1924.

———. *Kritik der neukantischen Rechtsphilosophie* [A critique of neo-Kantian legal philosophy]. Tübingen: Mohr, 1921.

———. "Staatslehre als theoretische Wissenschaft" [Political Theory as a Theoretical Discipline]. *Kantstudien* 31.1 (1926).

———. *Studien zur Staatslehre des monarchischen Prinzips* [Studies in the political theory of the monarchical principle]. Leipzig: Brandstetter, 1906.

———. *Das Wesen des Völkerrechts und die* Clausula rebus sic stantibus [The essence of international law and *clausula rebus sic stantibus*]. Tübingen: Mohr, 1911.

Kaufmann, Julius H. *Die Wertlosigkeit der Jurisprudenz als Wissenschaft* [The worthlessness of jurisprudence as a science]. Berlin: Springer, 1848.

Kelsen, Hans. *Allgemeine Staatslehre* [A general theory of the state]. Berlin: Springer, 1925.

———. "Der Begriff der Rechtserfahrung" [The concept of legal experience]. *Logos* 11 (1923): 285ff.

———. *Hauptprobleme der Staatsrechtslehre entwickelt aus der Lehre vom Rechtssatze* [Main problems of political theory, Developed from the theory of legal propositions]. Tübingen: Mohr, 1910. 2nd ed. 1923.

———. *Das Problem der Souveränität und die Theorie des Völkerrechts* [The problem of sovereignty and the theory of international Law]. Tübingen: Mohr, 1920.

———. "Die Rechtswissenschaft als Norm- oder als Kulturwissenschaft" [The science of law as a normative or cultural discipline]. *Schmollers Jahrbuch* (1916).

————. "Rechtswissenschaft und Recht" [The science of law and law]. *Zeitschrift für öffentliches Recht* II.1/2 (1922).

————. *Staat und Recht. Prolegomena zu einer Theorie der Rechtserfahrung* [State and law: Introduction to a theory of judicial process]. *Wiener Staatswissenschaftlichen Studien*, N. F., Vol. I (1922).

————. *Der soziologische und der juristische Staatsbegriff* [The Sociological and the Jural Concept of the State]. Tübingen: Mohr, 1922.

————. *Über Grenzen zwischen juristischer und soziologischer Methode* [The boundaries between the jural and sociological method]. Tübingen: Mohr, 1911.

————. "Über Staatsunrecht" [On state injustice]. *Grünhutszeitschrift für das Privat- und Öffentliches Recht* 40 (1913): 55.

————. "Das Verhältnis von Staat und Recht" [The relation between state and law]. *Archiv des öffentlichen Rechts*, New Series, 10.1/2 (1926): 153ff.).

————. *Vom Wesen und Wert der Demokratie* [On the essence and value of democracy]. Tübingen: Mohr, 1920.

————. "Zur Lehre vom öffentlichen Rechtsgeschäft" [Towards a theory of public legal action]. *Archiv des öffentlichen Rechts* 31 (1913): 69.

————. "Zur Methodik der Rechtswissenschaft" [On the method of the science of law]. *Kantstudien* 28.3/4 (1923): 283ff.

Klein, Franz. *Die psychischen Quellen des Rechtsgehorsams und der Rechtsgeltung* [The psychic sources of obedience to the law and legal validity]. Berlin: F. Vahlen, 1912.

Kohler, Josef. "Die Erforschung des Rechtsbewusztseins durch Beobachtung und Experiment" [Researching People's Sense of Justice by Means of Observation and Experiment]. *Juristenblätter*, 1912.

Kornfeld, Ignatz. *Soziale Machtverhältnisse* [Social power relationships]. Vienna: Manz, 1911.

Krabbe, Hugo. *De moderne Staatsidee*. The Hague: Martinus Nijhoff, 1915.

Kraepelin, Emil. Article in *Monatschrift für Kriminalpsychologie und Strafrechtsreform* 3 (1906): 269.

Kroner, Richard. *Von Kant bis Hegel*. 2 vols. Tübingen: Mohr, 1921, 1924.

Kuyper, A. *Het Calvinisme. Zes Stone-lezingen in October 1898 te Princeton (N.-J.) gehouden* [The Stone Lectures on Calvinism]. Amsterdam and Pretoria: Höveker & Wormser, 1899.

———. *Encyclopaedie der Heilige Godgeleerdheid* [Encyclopedia of sacred theology]. Vol. II, 2nd rev. ed. Kampen: Kok, 1909.

———. *Souvereiniteit in eigen kring* [Sphere sovereignty]. Kampen: Kok, 1880.

Landsberg, Ernst. *Geschichte der Deutschen Rechtswissenschaft* [A history of the science of law in Germany]. 3 vols. Munich and Leipzig: Oldenbourg, 1880–1910.

Lask, Emil. *Die Lehre vom Urteil* [The theory of judgment]. Tübingen: Mohr, 1912.

———. *Rechtsphilosophie.* In *Collected Works.* Tübingen: Mohr, 1923.

Leendertz, A. C. *De grond van het Overheidsgezag in de antirevolutionaire staatsleer* [The basis of governmental authority in the anti-revolutionary political theory]. Amsterdam: De Bussy, 1911.

Leibniz, G. W. *Gesammelte Werke.* Pertz-Gerhard ed. 4 vols. Hanover, 1843–47.

Lenz, Adolf. *Ein Strafgesetzbuch ohne Schuld und Strafe* [A penal code without guilt or punishment]. Univ. of Graz, 1922.

Maier, Heinrich. *An der Grenze der Philosophie: Melanchton, Lavater, David Friedrich Strauss.* Tübingen: Mohr, 1909.

Marck, Siegfried. *Substanz- und Funktionsbegriff in der Rechtsphilosophie* [The concepts of substance and function in legal philosophy]. Tübingen: Mohr, 1925.

Marx, Hermann. *Der Wissenschaftscharakter der Jurisprudenz* [The scientific nature of the science of law]. Berlin: De Gruyter, 1919.

Mayer, Max Ernst. *Rechtsphilosophie* [Philosophy of Law]. Berlin: Springer, 1922.

———. *"Rechtsphilosophie."* In *Encyclopädie der Rechts- und Staatswissenschaft,* Kohlrausch and Kaskel, eds. Berlin, 1922.

251

McDougall, William. *The Group Mind: A Sketch of the Principles of Collective Psychology with Some Attempts to Apply Them to the Interpretation of National Life and Character.* Cambridge University Press, U.K., 1920.

Meinecke, Friedrich. *Die Idee der Staatsräson in der neueren Geschichte.* Munich and Berlin: Oldenbourg, 1924. Eng. trans.: *Machiavellism: The Doctrine of Raison d'État and Its Place in Modern History.* New Haven, CT: Yale UP, 1957.

Merkl, Adolf. "Das doppelte Rechtsanlitz" [The double face of law]. *Juristische Blätter* 47 (1918).

———. *Die Lehre von der Rechtskraft, entwickelt aus dem Rechtsbegriff* [The theory of legal force, developed from the concept of law]. Leipzig and Vienna: Deuticke, 1923.

———. "Die Lehre von der Rechtskraft" [The theory of legal force]. *Wiener Staatswissenschaftlichen Studien* 15.2 (1923).

———. "Das Recht im Lichte seiner Anwendung" [Law in the light of its application]. *Deutsche Richterzeitung* 9 (1917).

Metzger, W. *Gesellschaft, Recht und Staat in der Ethik des Deutschen Idealismus* [Society, law and state in the ethics of German Idealism]. Heidelberg: Winter, 1917.

Natorp, Paul. *Die logischen Grundlagen der exakten Wissenschaften* [The logical foundations of the exact sciences]. 2nd ed. Leipzig: Teubner, 1921.

Nelson, Leonard. *Die Rechtswissenschaft ohne Recht* [The science of law without law]. Leipzig: Velt, 1917.

Nuszbaum, Arthur. Article in *Zeitschrift für Sozialwissenschaft* 9 (1906): 1–23.

Ofner, Julius. *Das Experiment im Recht* [Experiments in law]. 1882.

———. "Die naturwissenschaftliche Methode im Recht" [The natural-scientific method in law].

Oppenheim, Paul. *Die natürliche Ordnung der Wissenschaften* [The natural order of the sciences]. Jena: Fischer, 1926.

Oppenheimer, Franz. *System der Soziologie* [System of sociology]. Stuttgart: G. Fischer, 1922.

Ostwald, Wilhelm. *Energetische Grundlagen der Kulturwissenschaft* [The energetic foundations of the science of culture]. Leipzig: Klinkhardt, 1907.

Overbeck, Alfred Freiherr von. "Die Erscheinungsformen des Verbrechens im Lichte der modernen Strafrechtsschule" [The empirical forms of crime in light of the modern school of penal law]. In *Kritische Beiträge zur Strafrechtsreform* [Critical contributions to the reform of penal law]. Leipzig: Engelmann, 1909.

Petrazycki, Leon. *Über die Motive des Handelns und über das Wesen der Moral und des Rechts* [On the motives of action and the essence of morality and law]. Berlin: De Gruyter, 1907.

Petzoldt, Joseph. "Beseitigung der mengentheoretischen Paradoxa durch logisch einwandfreie Definition des Mengenbegriffs" [Sidestepping the paradoxes of set theory

through an unobjectionable definition of the set concept]."
Kantstudien 30 (1925): 346ff.

Post, Albert Hermann. *Grundrisz der Ethnologischen Jurisprudenz* [Outline of an ethnological jurisprudence]. 2 vols. Oldenburg: Schulze, 1894/95.

———. *Der Ursprung des Rechts* [The origin of law]. Oldenburg: Schulze, 1876.

Przywara, Erich. "Thomas oder Hegel." *Logos* 15.1. 1926.

Radbruch, Gustav. *Einführung in die Rechtswissenschaft* [Introduction to the science of law], 4th ed. (1919.

———. *Grundzüge der Rechtsphilosophie* [Fundamentals of legal philosophy]. Leipzig: Quelle und Meyer, 1914.

———. *Der Handlungsbegriff* [The act concept]. (Berlin: Guttentag, 1903.

———. "Die Problematik der Rechtsidee" [The problem concerning the idea of law]. *Jahrbuch für Geisteswissenschaften* 3 (1924).

———. "Rechtswissenschaft als Rechtsschöpfung" [The science of law as the creation of law]. *Archiv für Sozialwissenschaft*, Neue Folge, IV (1906): 355ff.

———. "Religionsphilosophie der Kultur," *Vorträge der Kantgesellschaft*.

———. "*Über den Begriff der Kultur*" [On the concept of culture]. *Logos* 11 (1920/21): 200ff.

Ratzenhofer, Gustav. *Die Kritik des Intellekts: Positive Erkenntnistheorie* [The critique of intellect: Positive epistemology]. Leipzig: Brockhaus, 1902.

————. *Positive Ethik: Die Verwirklichung des Sittlich-Seinsollenden* [Positive ethics: The realization of the Sein-Sollend]. Leipzig: Brockhaus. 1901.

————. *Der positive Monismus und das einheitliche Princip aller Erscheinungen* [Positive monism and the unified principle of all phenomena]. Leipzig: Brockhaus, 1899.

————. *Soziologische Erkenntnis* [Sociological knowledge]. Leipzig: Brockhaus. 1898.

————. *Wesen und Zweck der Politik als Theil der Soziologie und Grundlage der Staatswissenschaften* [The essence and aim of politics as part of sociology and the basis of the political sciences]. 3 vols. Leipzig: Brockhaus, 1893.

Reinach, Adolf. *Die apriorischen Grundlagen des bürgerlichen Rechtes* [The *a priori* foundations of civil law]. Halle an der Saale: Niemeyer, 1913.

Retslag, C. H. L. *Apologie der Jurisprudenz* [Apologia for the science of law]. Berlin: Braune, 1848.

Rickert, Heinrich. *Der Gegenstand der Erkenntnis* [The object of knowledge]. 3rd ed. Tübingen: Mohr, 1915.

————. *Die Grenzen der naturwissenschaftlichen Begriffsbildung* [The limits of concept formation in the natural sciences]. 2nd ed. 1913.

————. *Kulturwissenschaft und Naturwissenschaft* [Cultural science and natural science]. 5th ed. Tübingen: Mohr, 1921.

255

————. *System der Philosophie.* Tübingen: Mohr. 1921.

————. "Vom Begriff der Philosophie" [On the concept of philosophy]. *Logos* 1 (1910).

————. "Zwei Wege der Erkenntnistheorie" [Two directions in epistemology]. *Kantstudien* 14 (1909).

Rosenzweig, Franz. *Hegel und der Staat.* Vol. II. Munich: Oldenbourg, 1920.

Ross, Edward Alsworth. *The Principles of Sociology.* New York: Century, 1920.

Ruck, Erwin. *Die Leibniz'sche Staatsidee aus dem Quellen dargestellt* [The Leibniz idea of the state, developed from the sources]. Tübingen: Mohr, 1909.

Rudorff, A. F. *Kritik der Schrift des Staatsanwalts Von Kirchmann über die Werthlosigkeit der Jurisprudenz als Wissenschaft, von einem Lehrer dieser Wissenschaft* [A critique of Public Prosecutor Kirchmann's work on the uselessness of the science of law, by a teacher of this discipline]. Berlin: Plahn, 1848.

Rumpf, Max. *Volk und Recht* (Nation and law]. Oldenburg: Stalling, 1910.

Salomon, Max. *Grundlegung zur Rechtsphilosophie* [Grounding legal philosophy]. Berlin-Grunewald: Walther Rothschild, 1920.

Sander, Fritz. "Alte und neue Staatsrechtslehre" [The old and the new theory of constitutional law]. *Zeitung für öffentliches Recht* 2 (1921): 176ff.

———. "Das Faktum der Revolution und die Kontinuität der Rechtsordnung" [The *de facto* condition of revolution and the continuity of the legal order]. *Zeitung für öffentliches Recht* 1 (1919/20).

———. "Der Gegenstand der reinen Gesellschaftslehre" [The object of a pure theory of society]. *Archiv für Sozialwissenschaft und Sozialpolitik* 54.2 (1924): 329–423.

———. *Kelsens Rechtslehre: Kampfschrift wider die normativen Jurisprudenz* [Kelsen's legal theory: A polemic against the Normative School of Jurisprudence]. Tübingen: Mohr, 1923.

———. "Othmar Spanns Überwindung der individualistischen Gesellschaftsauffassung" [Othmar Spann's triumph over the individualistic view of society]. *Archiv für Sozialwissenschaft und Sozialpolitik* 53.1 (1923): 11–80.

———. "Rechtslehre oder Theorie der Rechtserfahrung? Kritische Studie zur Rechtslehre Hans Kelsens" [A theory of law or a theory of legal experience? A critical study of Kelsen's legal theory]. *Zeitschrift für öffentliches Recht* 2 (1921): 551–670.

———. "Staat und Recht als Probleme der Phänomenologie und Ontologie" [State and law as problems for phenomenology and ontology]. *Zeitschrift für öffentliches Recht* 4 (1924).

———. "Die transzendentale Methode der Rechtsphilosophie und der Begriff des Rechtsverfahrens" [The transcendental method of legal philosophy and the concept of legal action]. *Zeitung für öffentliches Recht* 1 (1919/20): 468ff.

———. "Das Verhältnis von Staat und Recht. Eine Grenzauseinandersetzung zwischen allgemeiner Staatslehre, theoretischer Rechtswissenschaft und interpretativer Rechtsdogmatik" [The relation between state and law: An inquiry into the boundaries between the general science of politics, the theoretical science of law, and interpretive systematic jurisprudence]. *Archiv des öffentlichen Rechts*, Neue Folge, 10.1/2 (1926): 153 ff.

———. "Zum Problem der Soziologie des Rechtes" [On the problem of the sociology of law]. *Archiv für Sozialwissenschaft und Sozialpolitik* 55.1 (1925).

Sauer, Wilhelm. *Grundlagen der Gesellschaft. Eine Rechts-, Staats- und Sozialphilosophie* [Foundations of society: A philosophy of law, state and society]. Berlin-Grunewald: Rothschild, 1924.

———. *Grundlagen der Wissenschaft und der Wissenschaften. Eine logische und sozialphilosophische Untersuchung* [Foundations of science and the disciplines: A logical and social philosophic investigation]. Berlin-Grunewald: Rothschild, 1926.

———. *Philosophie der Zukunft* [Philosophy of the future]. Stuttgart: Enke, 1926.

Savornin Lohman, A. F. de. *Over het hoogste gezag* [On the supreme authority]. Utrecht: Kemink, 1884.

Scheler, Max. *Der Genius des Krieges und der deutsche Krieg* [The genius of war and the German war]. 3rd ed. Leipzig: Verlag Weissen Bücher, 1915.

———. *Krieg und Aufbau* [War and construction].

Leipzig: Verlag Weissen Bücher, 1916.

Schmalenbach, Herman. *Leibniz.* Munich: Drei Masken, 1921.

Schmid, J. J. von. *Staatsrechtswetenschap en Sociologie* [The science of constitutional law and sociology]. Haarlem: Tjeenk Willink, 1926.

Schreier, Fritz. "Grundbegriffe und Grundformen des Rechts" [Basic concepts and basic forms of law]. *Wiener Staatswissenschaftliche Studien*, Neue Folge, 4 (1924).

Schuppe, Wilhelm. "Der Begriff des Rechts" [The concept of law]. *Grünhuts Zeitschrift für das privat- und öffentliches Recht* 10 (1883).

———. *Grundzüge der Ethik und Rechtsphilosophie* [Fundamentals of ethics and legal philosophy]. Breslau: Koebner, 1881.

Siegel, Carl. "Kant's antinomienlehre im Lichte der Inaugural Dissertation" [Kant's theory of antinomy in light of his inaugural dissertation]. *Kantstudien* 30.1/2 (1925): 67ff.

Sigwart, Christoph. *Kleine Schriften. Band 2.* Freiburg im Breisgau: Mohr, 1897.

Solvay, Ernest. *Industrie et Science.* Brussels: Solvay Institute for Sociology, 1910.

———. *Notes sur le Productivisme et le Comptabilisme.* Brussels: Solvay Institute, 1900.

———. *Principes de politique sociale (Questions d'énergétique sociale).* Brussels: Solvay Institute, 1901.

————. *Le productivisme social (Questions d'énergétique sociale)*. Brussels: Solvay Institute, 1894–1910.

————. *Science contre religion*. Brussels: Mayolez, 1879.

————. "Sur les Fondements positifs bio-psychiques et énergéto-productivistes de l'évolution sociale" [On the positive bio-psychical and productive energetical foundations of social evolution]. *Revue économique internationale* 10 (Dec. 1913).

————. *La Théorie des échanges et la Notion du productivisme sociale* [The theory of barter and the idea of social production]. Brussels: Solvay Institute, 1921.

Staffel, Walter. "Über Stammlers Lehre vom richtigen Recht" [On Stammler's theory of right law]. *Jahrbücher für die Dogmatik des heutigen römischen und deutschen Privatrechts*, vol. 49, 2nd series, XIII–XIV (1905).

Stahl, F. J. *Rechtswissenschaft oder Volksbewusztsein* [Legal science and national consciousness]. Berlin: Förstner, 1848.

Stammler, Rudolf. *Lehrbuch der Rechtsphilosophie* [Handbook of legal philosophy]. Berlin: De Gruyter, 1922.

————. *Theorie der Rechtswissenschaft* [Theory of the science of law]. Halle: Weisenhauses, 1911.

————. *Wirtschaft und Recht nach der materialistischen Geschichtsauffassung. Eine sozial-philosophische Untersuchung* [Economy and law according to the materialist view of history: A social-philosophical inquiry]. 3rd rev. ed. Leipzig: Von Veit, 1914.

Sternberg, Theo. *J. H. v. Kirchmann und seine Kritik der Rechtswissenschaft* [J. H. von Kirchmann and his Criticism of the Science of Law]. Berlin: Rothschild, 1908.

Sturm, August. *Die psychologische Grundlage des Rechts. Ein Beitrag zur allgemeinen Rechtslehre* [The psychological basis of law: A contribution to the science of law]. Hannover: Helwing, 1910.

Thomsen, Andreas. *Das Deutsche Strafrecht* [German penal law]. Berlin: Struppe & Winkler, 1907.

Tönnies, Ferdinand. *Thomas Hobbes, der Mann und der Denker.* 2nd enl. ed. Stuttgart: Frommann, 1922.

Vaihinger. "Zur Theorie der juristischen Fiktionen" [Towards a theory of juristic fictions]. *Annalen der Philosophie* I (1919): 630 ff.

Verdross, A. von. "Grundlagen und Grundlegungen des Völkerrechts" [Laying the foundations of international law]. *Niemeyer's Zeitschrift für Internationales Recht* 29 (1921): 65ff.

———. *Die Einheit des rechtlichen Weltbildes auf Grundlage des Völkerrechtsverfassung* [The unity of global law on the basis of prevailing international law]. Tübingen: Mohr, 1923.

———. "Zur Konstruktion des Völkerrechts" [Toward the construction of international law]. *Zeitschrift für Völkerrechts* 8 (1919): 329–359.

Vierkandt, Alfred. *Gesellschaftslehre. Hauptprobleme der Philosophischen Soziologie* [Theory of society: Main problems in philosophical sociology]. Stuttgart: Enke, 1923.

Weber, Max. "Die objektivität sozialwissenschaftlicher und sozialpolitischer Erkenntnis" [The objectivity of the knowledge of social science and social politics]. *Archiv für Sozialwissenschaft und Sozialpolitik* 19 (1904).

———. *R. Stammlers "Ueberwindung" der materialistischen Geschichtsauffassung"* [R. Stammler's "conquest" of the materialist view of history]. *Gesammelte Aufsätze zur Wissenschaftslehre* (1922), pp. 291–395, 556–579.

Wielikowski, G. A. *Die Neukantianer in der Rechtsphilosophie* [The neo-Kantians in legal philosophy]. Munich: Beck, 1914.

Wieser, Friedrich von. *Recht und Macht* [Law and power]. Leipzig: Duncker & Humblot, 1910.

Wilbrandt, Robert. "Max Weber als Erkenntniskritiker der Sozialwissenschaften" [Max Weber as critical epistemologist of the social sciences]. *Zeitschrift für die gesammte Staatswissenschaften* 79.4 (1925): 583–675.

Windelband, Wilhelm. *Geschichte und Naturwissenschaft* [History and natural science]. Strassburg: Heitz, 1894.

———. *Die Philosophie im Deutschen Geistesleben des XIX. Jahrhunderts* [Philosophy in the intellectual life of Germany during the 19th century]. Tübingen: Mohr, 1909.

Wust, Peter. *Die Auferstehung der Metaphysik* [The resurrection of metaphysics]. Leipzig: Meiner, 1920.

Zevenbergen, Willem. *Leerboek van het Nederlandsche Strafrecht* [Handbook of Dutch criminal law]. Groningen:

Wolters, 1924.

Zitelmann, Ernst. *Irrtum und Rechtsgeschäft. Eine psychologisch-juristische Untersuchung* [Error and legal acts: A psychological-juristic investigation]. Leipzig: Duncker & Humblot, 1879.

Index of Subjects

R

www.ingramcontent.com/pod-product-compliance
Lightning Source LLC
Chambersburg PA
CBHW030912120626
46554CB00001B/119